MISREADING RITUAL

MISREADING RITUAL

Sacrifice and Purity for the Modern-Day Gentile

ABBY KAPLAN

RESOURCE *Publications* • Eugene, Oregon

MISREADING RITUAL
Sacrifice and Purity for the Modern-Day Gentile

Copyright © 2022 Abby Kaplan. All rights reserved. Except for brief quotations in critical publications or reviews, no part of this book may be reproduced in any manner without prior written permission from the publisher. Write: Permissions, Wipf and Stock Publishers, 199 W. 8th Ave., Suite 3, Eugene, OR 97401.

Resource Publications
An Imprint of Wipf and Stock Publishers
199 W. 8th Ave., Suite 3
Eugene, OR 97401

www.wipfandstock.com

PAPERBACK ISBN: 978-1-6667-9912-5
HARDCOVER ISBN: 978-1-6667-9911-8
EBOOK ISBN: 978-1-6667-9913-2

MAY 11, 2022 10:20 AM

Except where otherwise noted, the scripture quotations contained herein are from the New Revised Standard Version Bible, copyright © 1989 by the Division of Christian Education of the National Council of the Churches of Christ in the U.S.A., and are used by permission. All rights reserved.

Some scripture quotations are from Revised Standard Version of the Bible, copyright © 1946, 1952, and 1971 National Council of the Churches of Christ in the United States of America. Used by permission. All rights reserved worldwide.

"The Heart of Worship," by Matt Redman, copyright © 1999 Thankyou Music (PRS) (adm. worldwide at CapitolCMGPublishing.com excluding the UK & Europe which is adm. at IntegratedRights.com). All rights reserved. Used by permission.

The Iliad, translated by Barry B. Powell, copyright © 2014 by Oxford University Press. Reproduced with permission of Oxford Publishing Limited through PLSclear.

גַּל־עֵינַי וְאַבִּיטָה נִפְלָאוֹת מִתּוֹרָתֶךָ

Open my eyes, so that I may behold
wondrous things out of your law.

PSALM 119:18

Contents

Acknowledgments | ix

List of Abbreviations | xi

1   Statutes That Were Not Good | 1

2   How I Love Your Law! | 14

3   What Sacrifice Is Not | 27

4   Sin Is like Dirt; Blood Is like Soap | 44

5   Not All Sacrifices Are about Sin | 57

6   Not All Dirt Is Sin | 78

7   The Purpose of Ritual Purity | 103

8   Food Laws | 119

9   Brothers, What Shall We Do? | 132

Bibliography | 135

General Index | 143

Scripture Index | 147

Acknowledgments

I'VE BEEN THINKING ABOUT Leviticus for a very long time—ever since 2011, when I first encountered Jacob Milgrom's Anchor Bible commentary. This book grew out of a series of classes and Bible studies that I've led since then; I owe a debt of gratitude to everyone who has tolerated—or, perhaps unwisely, encouraged—this idiosyncratic interest over the years. None of these generous people would necessarily agree with every conclusion in this book; all errors and missteps are mine alone.

Thanks, first of all, to all those who have participated in Bible studies on various Leviticus-related topics: Andy Abel, Jim and Judy Brown, Jim and Yanping Calvert, Becky Cannon, Chris Cassity, Linda Cottam, Linda Dennis, Stacy Eddings, Joy and Stephen Ennis, Dave Gayer, Joanna Graft, Dolores Hillaire, David and Jerri Hurley, Raymond and Susan Jew, LeeAnn Oliverson, Duona Richard, Sharon Rogers, Karen Sewell, John and Lesa Smith, Bryan and Meg Sours, Sharlean and Steve Thomsen, Timbra Wiist, and Tim Woodroof.

Brett McCarty, the staff at the Salt Lake City Public Library, and the staff at the Harold B. Lee Library of BYU went above and beyond the call of duty in helping me get access to hard-to-find books.

Special thanks to Allison Hamm, Ryne Parrish, Sally Rodriguez, and John Shoun for their thoughtful comments on the full manuscript. This book is much better because of them. Thanks also to Anna Kaplan for wise advice on the broader context of the book.

My parents, John and Carol Shoun, cultivated a home with a high view of scripture but where questions were always encouraged. I was similarly blessed to encounter the same environment at Cole Mill Road Church

ACKNOWLEDGMENTS

of Christ, Campbell Church of Christ, Cross Tower Church of Christ, and Murray Park Church of Christ.

My sons, Graham and Jay, were awesome Merarites and Gershonites when we needed help setting up the tent every week for a Leviticus class. Graham, in classic preteen fashion, even came to one class despite a warning that it would be gross. Jay has enthusiastically started calling Jesus the "goat of God."

Finally, Aaron is the best and most supportive husband a person could have. He's brilliant, thoughtful, and fun, and has never once complained about the inordinate amount of our shelf space now occupied by books on menstruation and ritual slaughter. I hit the jackpot!

List of Abbreviations

1 En.	1 Enoch
1QS	Rule of the Community
AB	Anchor Bible
Adv. Jud.	John Chrysostom, *Discourses against Judaizing Christians*
Agr.	Philo, *On Agriculture*
A.J.	Josephus, *Jewish Antiquities*
AJSR	*Association for Jewish Studies Review*
Anab.	Xenophon, *Anabasis*
ANET	*Ancient Near Eastern Texts Relating to the Old Testament.* Edited by James B. Pritchard. 3rd ed. Princeton: Princeton University Press, 1969.
AOTC	Abingdon Old Testament Commentaries
ApOTC	Apollos Old Testament Commentary
Argon.	Apollonius of Rhodes, *Argonautica*
ASOR	American Schools of Oriental Research
b. Ber.	Babylonian Talmud, tractate Berakhot
B.J.	Josephus, *Jewish War*
b. Nid.	Babylonian Talmud, tractate Niddah
BDB	Francis Brown, S. R. Driver, and Charles A. Briggs. *A Hebrew and English Lexicon of the Old Testament.* Oxford: Clarendon, 1907.

List of Abbreviations

BJS	Brown Judaic Studies
BRev	*Bible Review*
BSR	*Bulletin for the Study of Religion*
CAD	*The Assyrian Dictionary of the Oriental Institute of the University of Chicago*. Edited by Ignace J. Gelb, et al. 21 vols. Chicago: The Oriental Institute of the University of Chicago, 1956–2006.
CEJL	Commentaries on Early Jewish Literature
ChrCent	*The Christian Century*
Dial.	Justin Martyr, *Dialogue with Trypho*
DSSSE	*The Dead Sea Scrolls: Study Edition*. Edited and translated by Florentino García Martínez and Eibert J. C. Tigchelaar. 2nd ed. 2 vols. Leiden: Brill, 1999.
ER	*The Encyclopedia of Religion*. 16 vols. Edited by Mircea Eliade. New York: Macmillan, 1987.
Hist.	Herodotus, *Histories*
HTR	*Harvard Theological Review*
Il.	Homer, *Iliad*
JAAR	*Journal of the American Academy of Religion*
JAOS	*Journal of the American Oriental Society*
JBL	*Journal of Biblical Literature*
JQR	*The Jewish Quarterly Review*
JSJ	*Journal for the Study of Judaism in the Persian, Hellenistic, and Roman Periods*
JSNTSup	Journal for the Study of the New Testament Supplement Series
LCC	Library of Christian Classics
LCL	Loeb Classical Library
LEC	Library of Early Christianity
Legat.	Philo, *On the Embassy to Gaius*
Let. Aris.	*Letter of Aristeas*

List of Abbreviations

Lev. Rab.	*Leviticus Rabbah*
m. Ber.	Mishnah, tractate Berakhot
m. Hag.	Mishnah, tractate Hagigah
m. Ker.	Mishnah, tractate Kerithot
m. Naz.	Mishnah, tractate Nazir
m. Nid.	Mishnah, tractate Niddah
m. Pesah.	Mishnah, tractate Pesahim
m. Yad.	Mishnah, tractate Yadayim
m. Yoma	Mishnah, tractate Yoma
MC	Mesopotamian Civilizations
Migr.	Philo, *On the Migration of Abraham*
Mos.	Philo, *On the Life of Moses*
Nat.	Pliny the Elder, *Natural History*
NICOT	New International Commentary on the Old Testament
NPNF2	*Nicene and Post-Nicene Fathers*, Series 2. Edited by Philip Schaff and Henry Wace. 14 vols. Reprint, Grand Rapids: Eerdmans, 1976–1978.
PG	Patrologia Graeca. Edited by J.-P. Migne. 162 vols. Paris, 1857–1886.
RB	*Revue biblique*
RBS	Resources for Biblical Study
SAC	Studies in Antiquity and Christianity
Sacr.	Lucian, *Sacrifices*
SBLDS	Society for Biblical Literature Dissertation Series
SFSHJ	South Florida Studies in the History of Judaism
SNTSMS	Society for New Testament Studies Monograph Series
Spec.	Philo, *On the Special Laws*
t. Demai	Tosefta, tractate Demai
t. Yoma	Tosefta, tractate Yoma

List of Abbreviations

TDNT *Theological Dictionary of the New Testament.* 10 vols. Edited by Gerhard Kittel and Gerhard Friedrich. Translated by Geoffrey W. Bromiley. Grand Rapids: Eerdmans, 1964–1976.

TOTC Tyndale Old Testament Commentaries

y. Ketub. Jerusalem Talmud, tractate Ketubbot

YJS Yale Judaica Series

1

STATUTES THAT WERE NOT GOOD

ONE OF THE MOST STUNNING statements in the Bible is found in the book of Ezekiel. The prophet, preaching to fellow Jews living in exile in Babylon, retells the story of their ancestors wandering in the wilderness. But he doesn't tell a triumphant story of God freeing the slaves from Egypt and creating a holy people. Instead, he tells a tragic story of people who reject God over and over again. Ezekiel's point is that they're in exile now because they repeated the rebellious patterns of their ancestors.

So far, Ezekiel is in good company. Psalm 106 describes the wilderness wandering in a similar way, and plenty of the stories in Exodus and Numbers aren't exactly flattering. What *is* unique is what God says about the laws he gave to the Israelites:

> Moreover I gave them statutes that were not good and ordinances by which they could not live.[1]

This is a jaw-dropping claim. Is God really saying that he gave the Israelites bad laws? On purpose? What kind of god would do such a thing? And how do we reconcile this passage with, say, the book of Deuteronomy, which is chock-full of passages that say God's commandments are life-giving and good?

> If you obey the commandments of the LORD your God that I am commanding you today, by loving the LORD your God, walking in his ways, and observing his commandments, decrees, and

---

1. Ezek 20:25.

ordinances, then you shall live and become numerous, and the LORD your God will bless you in the land that you are entering to possess.[2]

In context, I think the most likely explanation for Ezekiel is that God was referring to child sacrifice. There's evidence that child sacrifice was practiced in ancient Israel, not least the fact that Jeremiah and Ezekiel spent a lot of time railing against it. The very next verse in the Ezekiel passage refers to "their offering up all their firstborn, in order that I might horrify them."[3] This sounds a lot like God "giving them up" to experience the consequences of their actions, Romans-style.[4]

This is a plausible way to understand the passage, even if it's not the only possibility.[5] What I *don't* find plausible is the idea that Ezekiel was saying the Torah itself is "not good." But, as it turns out, some commentators have come to precisely this conclusion. Aphrahat, a fourth-century Persian Christian, used Ezekiel to argue that Jewish ritual practices were objectively terrible:

> For now the mouth of the Holy One has testified that the commandments and the judgments which are given to you are not useful and are not excellent.... When they made for themselves the calf and turned away from him, *then* he gave them commandments and judgments which are not excellent: sacrifice, the purification of lepers, of discharge, of menstruation, and of childbirth; and that a man should not come near the dead, the grave, bones, and those who have been killed; that for all sins one must bring a sacrifice and for all uncleanness in man.... Truly through these matters which are written, Israel has not a single day of purity from sins, but all their days are spent in sins and in uncleanness.[6]

Aphrahat wasn't alone. From Justin Martyr[7] in the second century to Jean LeClerc[8] in the seventeenth century and beyond, commentators have argued that some Old Testament laws—usually the "ritual" laws about

---

2. Deut 30:16.
3. Ezek 20:26.
4. Rom 1:28.
5. Maccoby, "Statutes."
6. Aphrahat, *Demonstrations* 15.8.
7. Justin Martyr, *Dial.* 21–22.
8. LeClerc, *Libri Quatuor*, 627.

Statutes That Were Not Good

sacrifice and purity—are bad. Not just incomplete, not just a shadow of the better things inaugurated by Jesus, but truly, fundamentally bad.

Why would God give bad laws? Sometimes the argument is that the Jews are an especially sinful and perverse people, and these onerous commandments were the only appropriate discipline. All this, of course, is bound up with the shameful history of Christian anti-Semitism.[9] But even though some of the early church fathers' ideas wouldn't be acceptable in polite company today, it's not hard to find modern Christians agreeing that all that Old Testament stuff was just the worst.

One flavor of this line of thinking goes something like this: all those laws about sacrifices, ritual purity, and dietary restrictions were *intended* to be burdensome. God wanted to make people acutely aware of how sinful and imperfect they were; that way, Jesus' message of grace and freedom would seem even better by comparison.

Frankly, this doesn't sound like God. I have a hard time imagining God waiting for Moses on Mount Sinai, cackling with glee and exclaiming, "Oh, they're going to hate these laws so much! They'll *really* appreciate Jesus one day." But the view I've just described—admittedly in an uncharitable way—isn't all that far off from what you can find in some sincere interpretations of the Old Testament. Take, for example, the following discussion from a commentary on Leviticus aimed at children:

> The frustration my young friend experienced in trying to read Leviticus was not wrong; in fact, I believe it was part of what God intended. Let the truth be told: The many laws in Leviticus are definitely tedious! . . . [A]ll the ceremonial laws of Leviticus were a hard burden and heavy yoke under which the people staggered and fainted (Acts 15:10). . . . Thus we see another great purpose of Leviticus: By presenting the yoke and the burden and the barrier of the Law, this book provides a stark contrast to the grace of the New Covenant in Christ's blood. . . .[10]

Other Christians argue, not that the law was supposed to make Jesus look better by comparison, but that its goal was to give people an accurate understanding of just how bad sin is. I agree that the sacrificial system has a vital theology of sin, but I disagree with a popular next step in this line of reasoning: to take the book of Hebrews, which describes how Jesus

---

9. Ruether, *Faith and Fratricide.*
10. Ganz, *Leviticus.*

accomplished what the law couldn't, and conclude that ancient Israelites pretty much felt awful all the time.

> [T]he Israelites never felt free from the condemnation of past sins. In fact, "there is a remembrance again made of sins every year" [Hebrews 10:3]. On Yom Kippur (the day of atonement), sacrifices were offered, bringing to remembrance (calling to mind) the sins that the Israelites had committed. Yet in their hearts they knew that these sacrifices could not remove sin.[11]

What this book is about

I wrote this book because I want to push back against what is, in my opinion, an overly negative attitude towards Old Testament law in some Christian circles. In my experience, extreme statements like the ones we've just seen are rare, but *positive* assessments are even rarer. At best, the law codes in the Pentateuch suffer from benign neglect. When they do come up, it's usually with a devout but cursory "Thank God we don't have to do that anymore!" and no attempt to explore what these practices might have meant to those who lived them. Or we read Jesus criticizing how some of his contemporaries interpreted the law, and we dismiss the whole system as legalistic and outdated.

I find this state of affairs problematic for several reasons. First, the consistent witness of scripture is that the law is good. If it were otherwise, the exhausting 176 verses of Psalm 119 would be incomprehensible. The book of Ezekiel, 20:25 notwithstanding, is unabashedly pro-law. You can hardly turn around in the Old Testament without running into another passage that praises the law. If that's the story scripture is trying to tell, we should take it seriously. (And if you're thinking, "Wait, what about the New Testament?"—just hang on for a couple pages.)

Second, even if, as Christians believe, Jesus has brought something better than the law, that doesn't mean the law was intended to be bad, or that faithful Jews universally experienced it as bad. In-person worship services may be better than remote worship services by videoconference, but that doesn't mean virtual church is *intended* to be bad. Just the opposite! Churches offer online worship because they want to offer something *good* when worshipping in person isn't possible. And even if in-person worship is better, that doesn't mean no one ever finds joy or meaning online.

---

11. Levy, *Tabernacle*, 199–200.

Finally, if Old Testament law is nothing but a burden, then the obvious implication is that modern Jews who follow it are either masochists or fools. Not only is this conclusion an unpromising start to interfaith dialogue, but it's simply not true. The history of Jewish interpretation and practice is long and rich; it is, from a Christian perspective, precisely what faithful worshippers of God *should* be doing if Jesus hadn't come. Christians and Jews read scripture differently, and that's okay; we can start from the premise that others are acting in good faith, even if we don't agree. And Christians should have an extra incentive to listen to their Jewish brothers and sisters: if we want to understand what it would look like to meet God in the Old Testament day in and day out, as *all* followers of the Hebrew God did before Jesus, then the synagogue down the street isn't a bad place to start.

I want this book to offer a constructive reading of Old Testament law to Christians who usually skip over Leviticus. I'm specifically focused on three areas: sacrifice, ritual purity, and dietary regulations. These are the laws that Christians are least likely to take seriously—sometimes on the grounds that they're "ritual laws," as opposed to the "moral laws" that still apply today. (This despite the fact that the distinction between "ritual" and "moral" law is one that scripture itself doesn't make!) If this book prevents just one sermon about how sacrifice was supposed to make the Israelites feel guilty all the time, or just one Bible study remark that Jesus was more advanced than his fellow Jews because he saw that the purity laws were stupid, it's done its job.

But what about the New Testament?

Before we can truly get started on the Old Testament, we need to pause for a moment to talk about the *New* Testament. These negative views of the law don't come from nowhere; in fact, Christians have some very good reasons to view certain practices with a critical eye. Don't the words of Jesus and Paul demand that we disavow sacrifice, ritual, and everything that went with it?

Well, not exactly. Yes, the New Testament is clear that the death of Jesus means sacrifices are no longer necessary, and that God doesn't require Christians to follow the laws about ritual purity or dietary restrictions. But that's different from saying that these things were never worthy of respect in the first place, or that their only purpose was punitive, or that they were universally hated.

Misreading Ritual

Essentially, there are two major motifs in the New Testament that ought to discourage a knee-jerk dismissal of these laws. First is the fact that Jesus showed respect for the law's authority, and other figures in the New Testament did the same. When he healed lepers, he instructed them to follow the ritual procedures described in Leviticus.[12] (And, contrary to popular belief, Jesus wasn't breaking the law when he touched lepers or dead bodies; more on this in chapter 6.) It's likely that Jesus entered Jerusalem a week before Passover in order to undergo purification rituals himself.[13] The disputes between Jesus and other religious leaders weren't about whether the Old Testament law itself was valid; rather, they had rival *interpretations* of that law. Jesus disagreed with some of his contemporaries about how to keep the Sabbath,[14] but not about the institution of Sabbath itself. He condemned backwards priorities, but his point was that some things mattered *less*, not that they mattered *nothing*:

> Woe to you, scribes and Pharisees, hypocrites! For you tithe mint, dill, and cummin, and have neglected the weightier matters of the law: justice and mercy and faith. It is these you ought to have practiced *without neglecting the others*.[15]

Similarly, Jesus assumed that his followers were going to offer sacrifices, and he didn't seem to have a problem with this.

> So when you are offering your gift at the altar, if you remember that your brother or sister has something against you, leave your gift there before the altar and go; first be reconciled to your brother or sister, *and then come and offer your gift.*[16]

Jesus could have said, "Go be reconciled to your brother or sister; you can forget about the offering, because it didn't matter anyway." But he didn't. Again, he respected the institution of sacrifice, even while he insisted that it wasn't of first importance. Jesus claimed authority to interpret the law,[17] but he also insisted that "I have come not to abolish [the law] but to fulfill."[18]

---

12. Matt 8:2–4 // Mark 1:40–44 // Luke 5:12–14; Luke 17:12–14.
13. Fredriksen, "Did Jesus Oppose?," 43.
14. Mark 2:23–28 // Luke 6:1–5; Mark 3:1–5; Luke 13:10–17; 14:1–6; John 5:2–17.
15. Matt 23:23, emphasis added.
16. Matt 5:23–24, emphasis added.
17. Matt 5:21–48.
18. Matt 5:17.

Statutes That Were Not Good

Even the apostle Paul, who argued passionately that we are set right by Jesus and not by observing the law, could refer to the law as "holy and just and good"[19] and conclude, "Do we then overthrow the law by this faith? By no means! On the contrary, we uphold the law."[20]

The second motif, closely related to the first one, is that keeping the Old Testament law—including the parts that some Christians dismiss as pointless legalism—was clearly *attractive* to many Jews. We'll see many more examples in chapter 2; for now, just consider the fact that if everyone hated following the law, Paul probably wouldn't have had to spend so much time writing letters about how parts of it were no longer necessary. And Hebrews was clearly written to Christians who were attracted to Judaism. A long section of Hebrews is devoted to explaining how Jesus was the sacrifice to end all sacrifices;[21] to me, the letter sounds less like "now you can stop worrying about all those terrible sacrifices you've always hated" and more like "you know all those things you love about sacrifices? Jesus does them even better!"

To sum up: Even if Jesus brought something better than the law, even if God always meant for the law to be temporary, even if the law bowed its authority to Jesus—none of this has to mean that the law was intrinsically bad. The story of the controversy over the Sabbath, as told in the gospel of Matthew, summarizes things well:

> At that time Jesus went through the grainfields on the sabbath; his disciples were hungry, and they began to pluck heads of grain and to eat. When the Pharisees saw it, they said to him, "Look, your disciples are doing what is not lawful to do on the sabbath." He said to them, "Have you not read what David did when he and his companions were hungry? He entered the house of God and ate the bread of the Presence, which it was not lawful for him or his companions to eat, but only for the priests. Or have you not read in the law that on the sabbath the priests in the temple break the sabbath and yet are guiltless? I tell you, something greater than the temple is here. But if you had known what this means, 'I desire mercy and not sacrifice,' you would not have condemned the guiltless. For the Son of Man is lord of the sabbath."[22]

---

19. Rom 7:12.
20. Rom 3:31.
21. Heb 8:1—10:25.
22. Matt 12:1–8.

As usual, the context is a dispute about how to interpret the law. "I desire mercy and not sacrifice" is a quote from the prophet Hosea. You could read this verse in strict binary terms: God wants mercy and does *not* want sacrifice. But this "X, not Y" frame doesn't have to have that meaning. Compare the proverb "Take my correction and not silver, knowledge instead of choice gold."[23] This proverb most likely isn't encouraging us to avoid money entirely. Rather, the point is that instruction and knowledge are *more important than* silver and gold.[24] This interpretation perfectly fits the story in Matthew, where Jesus observes that "something greater than the temple is here."

So then, if Christians want to follow the example of Jesus, we ought to be willing to sit at the feet of Moses for a while. This doesn't mean that we have to give up a distinctively Christian interpretation of the Old Testament, but it does mean that we shouldn't be too quick to rush to the end of the story.

The arrogance of evolutionism

I've just argued that we can show respect to ancient Israelite religious practices even from an unabashedly Christian perspective. That is, even if we believe that sacrifices aren't necessary after Jesus, we can still try to understand what sacrifice meant to people who hadn't yet read the end of the story, so to speak. And we can do this without assuming that pre-Jesus Judaism was perpetually sad (because the rules were so burdensome) or Christian in all but name (because the truly faithful had figured out how the story was going to end). That said, there's one more line of thought that we need to be careful about.

In religious studies, the term "evolutionism" primarily refers to a type of theorizing that was popular in the late nineteenth and early twentieth centuries.[25] The idea was that human societies naturally progress from "primitive" ideas about the divine to more "advanced" ideas, and that this evolution happens in a linear, universal pattern. Usually these primitive ideas are supposed to be magical or literal, and later generations improve on those ideas by metaphorizing or spiritualizing them. Evolutionist theories

23. Prov 8:10, my translation.
24. Rofé, *Prophetic Literature*, quoted in Klawans, *Symbolism and Supersessionism*, 81.
25. Waller and Edwardsen, "Evolutionism," 214–18.

have the major advantage that they provide a Grand Unified Theory of Religion, and the slight drawback that they're all wrong. Actual religious practices across cultures, and the ways those practices change over time, just don't follow the neat and orderly progression that evolutionist theories say they should.

Evolutionism also tends to give ourselves too much credit and other groups too little. It's a remarkable coincidence that the "highest" level of development in a given evolutionist theory often looks a lot like the values and practices of the person who proposed that theory. Conversely, we see a tendency to assume that ancient people were incapable of interpreting their religious practices as symbolic or metaphorical, which is absolutely untrue. Plenty of ancient writers criticized what modern thinkers might call "primitive" ideas. Lucian of Samosata, writing in the second century, mocked transactional views of sacrifice:

> In view of what the dolts do at their sacrifices and their feasts and processions in honour of the gods, what they pray for and vow, and what opinions they hold about the gods, I doubt if anyone is so gloomy and woe-begone that he will not laugh to see the idiocy of their actions. Indeed, long before he laughs, I think, he will ask himself whether he should call them devout or, on the contrary, irreligious and pestilent, inasmuch as they have taken it for granted that the gods are so low and mean as to stand in need of men and to enjoy being flattered and to get angry when they are slighted. . . .
>
> So nothing, it seems, that [the gods] do is done without compensation. They sell men their blessings, and one can buy from them health, it may be, for a calf, wealth for four oxen, a royal throne for a hundred, a safe return from Troy to Pylos for nine bulls, and a fair voyage from Aulis to Troy for a king's daughter! Hecuba, you know, purchased temporary immunity for Troy from Athena for twelve oxen and a frock. One may imagine, too, that they have many things on sale for the price of a cock or a wreath or nothing more than incense.[26]

Critiques like those don't necessarily mean that Lucian was a nonconformist who stood off to the side while all his contemporaries went on sacrificing. On the contrary: ancient writers were perfectly capable of accepting sacrifice as an institution—and practicing it themselves—while debating exactly what it meant or how it should be done.[27] Imagine a

---

26. Lucian, *Sacr.* 1–2.
27. Ullucci, *Christian Rejection*, 34–56.

Christian preacher thundering at his congregation for doing prayer all wrong: they expect to get what they pray for automatically, as though God were a heavenly vending machine. We don't necessarily expect that the preacher is about to evolve beyond the primitive practice of prayer; rather, the preacher accepts prayer as a good thing and wants it done properly.

Full-blown evolutionist theories are out of fashion today (at least in academic circles), but there's still plenty of evolutionist reasoning in the air.[28] To take just one example, Rob Bell's commentary on Leviticus is shot through with evolutionist language.[29] Animal sacrifice, in his telling, was an advance over the sacrificial practices of Israel's neighbors; even though it was still "primitive" and "barbaric," it has a lot to teach us today, but society has "evolved" beyond the need to engage in literal sacrifice anymore. To be fair, Bell is trying to address the concerns of people who are horrified by the very idea of animal sacrifice; some of his use of this language is intended to acknowledge those feelings. (And Bell regularly acknowledges ways in which our modern practices may well be *worse* than those of our forebears.) But the overall scheme is still strongly evolutionist.

Another idea with evolutionist flavor, one that's extremely popular in some Christian circles, comes from the work of René Girard.[30] Girard was a literary critic who argued that sacrifice originated as a solution to human violence. Rival groups naturally engage in cycles of violent retaliation, and they break the cycle by channeling all that violence onto an innocent third-party victim (a "scapegoat"). Crucially, the scapegoating mechanism works only if we don't recognize that the victim is innocent—that is, only if all the former enemies are united in the delusion that we're punishing the one responsible for our problems. Sacrifice is a ritualized version of this process; it's unjust but effective (because it reduces interpersonal violence). Jesus' death was an example of scapegoating, but it's different from all other examples because the innocence of the victim was clearly revealed; this breaks open the unjust system and shows it for what it is. That's how Jesus saves us: by exploding our violent system from the inside and preventing us from creating any more scapegoats.

Girard's ideas are often seen as an alternative to penal substitutionary atonement; that is, they let us explain how Jesus' death saves us without

---

28. Klawans, *Symbolism and Supersessionism*, 17–48; Sacks, *Leviticus*, 71–77, 101–8, 115–22.
29. Bell, "Blood, Guts, & Fire."
30. Girard, *Violence and the Sacred*.

appealing to an angry God who punished Jesus instead of us. (For more on this, see chapter 3.) As far as that goes, I'm a fan. The concept of the scapegoating mechanism is an excellent tool for doing theology—it gives us one more picture for understanding what Jesus' death means, one that complements other images of cleansing, identification, conquering the powers of darkness, and so on.

But Girard didn't just claim that the cross (properly understood) means the end of violence. He claimed that all sacrifice, everywhere, is *actually* a scapegoating mechanism in disguise. Even if the people doing the sacrifice think it's about something else—for example, sharing a meal with a deity—that just proves that they've successfully hidden the innocent scapegoat. Girard's critics respond that his theory is unfalsifiable: if some sacrificial ritual doesn't look like the theory claims it should, well, that means the scapegoat is disguised, which is more evidence for the theory![31]

Aside from the empirical question (can we really *know* that all sacrificial rituals can be traced back to some ancient scapegoating event?), Girard's approach implies that we have nothing to learn from sacrifice or those who practice it. Sacrifice is irredeemably violent, so the best course is to run away from it as fast as possible. And the innocent scapegoat is always disguised, so there's no use listening to what practitioners say they're doing; they're just fooling themselves anyway. Therefore, we ought to dismiss all sacrifice out of hand, without even giving it a hearing. Followers of Girard have argued that Jesus' action in the temple was a repudiation of all sacrifice,[32] and even that Jesus encountered a demon-possessed man at a synagogue because "[r]eligion as usual is the place of the demonic, and Jesus is the enemy of both."[33]

There's certainly an argument to be made that killing animals for human purposes is inherently inhumane—but I'm far from the first person to point out that if we're outraged by animal sacrifice, we ought to be outraged many times over by the modern meat industry. If we grant that, say, a Christmas turkey dinner can have meaning for its participants beyond the death of a bird (family connection, for example), then surely we can do the same for sacrifice. There's no logical contradiction between acknowledging the positive aspects of a ritual while preferring something else.

---

31. Klawans, "Something Bigger," 23–27.

32. Matt 21:12–13 // Mark 11:15–17 // Luke 19:45–46 // John 2:13–16; Hamerton-Kelly, *Poetics of Violence*, 15–19.

33. Mark 1:21–26; Hamerton-Kelly, *Poetics of Violence*, 75.

I've already argued that Christians can, and should, be respectful students of the Old Testament while still reading it in a distinctively Christian way. In that sense, even this book is unavoidably a bit evolutionist, or at least supersessionist. But in what follows, I've tried to avoid some of the pitfalls we've just seen: assuming an inevitable, natural progression towards "better" religion; attributing foreign-seeming practices to unsophisticated ancient minds; certainty that we moderns have everything figured out.

Engaging with Jewish interpreters

One last note before we really get started. If our goal is to spend some time living in the world of Old Testament law, then we ought to learn from others who have done so before us. And those voices, of course, include ancient and modern Jewish sources. As many other Christian writers have done, this book cites the work of Jewish thinkers from around the time of Jesus (Philo and Josephus), the first few centuries thereafter (the Mishnah and the Talmud), the Middle Ages (e.g., Maimonides), and beyond.

Just a few words of caution are in order, especially with regard to older works. First, none of these writers can tell us about actual practices in Israel before the first temple was destroyed; even the earliest of them were written hundreds of years later. Second, we should be extremely careful before assuming that these writers can tell us about actual practices even in the time of the *second* temple. The Mishnah was compiled over a hundred years after the second temple was destroyed; although it contains oral traditions that are much older, it's extremely difficult to discern which statements describe what people were actually doing at an earlier time, and which statements are later interpretations. Finally, no single writer represents The Jewish Position on a given topic. Judaism, like any other religious tradition, has and always has had a great diversity of thought and practice. The Mishnah itself records disagreements explicitly: "Hillel says this; Shammai says that." Imagine asking one random Christian about the meaning of, say, baptism, and assuming that her answer represents all Christians everywhere!

For the most part, my interest is not to use these writings to reconstruct daily Jewish life thousands of years ago—that's a job for historians. Rather, they tell us about what some Jewish writers believed. If we want to know how the Old Testament might speak to us today, it's worth listening to how it has spoken to others who spent a lifetime living and wrestling faithfully with the text.

I want to acknowledge my own biases, and for that reason I use the term "Old Testament" to refer to the collection of writings also known as the "Hebrew Bible." The latter term is often used as a way of acknowledging that Christians aren't the only ones who read these texts as scripture; being clear on this point is good and necessary, especially for Christians who may be unaware that Jewish interpretation didn't stop in AD 33! But I've chosen the former term here in order to be up-front about the fact that this book is written from a Christian perspective, and that perspective will naturally color the way I read these texts. In other words, of the Jewish writings about the Old Testament, I take as authoritative those that reflect on what it meant in the light of Jesus—that is, the *New* Testament. This means I'll be taking other Jewish commentators' ideas in directions they themselves wouldn't necessarily agree with; we would be fooling ourselves to pretend otherwise. I believe it's possible to stay rooted in one faith tradition while engaging respectfully with others, and I hope I've accomplished that here.

Last point. The name "Kaplan" is common among Ashkenazi Jews, so I should take a moment to acknowledge that I am not, in fact, Jewish. My husband is. I can't claim any special knowledge of contemporary Judaism, other than what I happen to have seen among my in-laws—among whom, as in any family, there's a whole variety of practices. (My husband himself grew up celebrating Passover and Chanukkah, but not keeping kosher or attending synagogue.) If you bought this book hoping to learn about sacrifice and purity laws from an authoritative Jewish source, I apologize.

Roadmap

Chapter 2 contains the other half of the argument begun in this chapter. The story the Old Testament tells is one in which ancient Israelites, far from feeling that all the sacrifices were a burden, actually *liked* them. Chapters 3, 4, and 5 develop an interpretation of the various types of sacrifices found in Leviticus. Chapters 6 and 7 move on to the ritual purity laws, and chapter 8 concludes with a discussion of dietary regulations.

I firmly believe that these strange-looking laws have something positive to teach, even to those of us who live in a society very different from the world in which they were written. In the words of sixteenth-century commentator Johannes Brenz: Lucian laughs at sacrifice, but the Holy Spirit laughs back.[34]

---

34. Brenz, *In Leviticum Librum*, 6; quoted in Elliott, *Engaging Leviticus*, 1.

2

HOW I LOVE YOUR LAW!

> Oh, how I love your law!
> It is my meditation all day long.
>
> Ps 119:97

Whose idea was sacrifice?

I HAVE NEVER PARTICIPATED in animal sacrifice. And if I wanted to, I wouldn't even know how to get started. (Are there any altars in my city, or would I have to build my own? Where would I get an animal? Would I be in danger of violating any laws? Not to mention the fact that I have zero training as a butcher.)

I'm not alone; for those of us who live in cultures far removed from these kinds of practices, sacrifice is completely foreign. When we read Leviticus, with its extensive laws on sacrificial rituals, a natural reaction is to ask, "Why did God command all this?" Plenty of commentaries addressed to modern audiences try to answer the question:

> As people continued to rebel against God's laws, He gave them a plan to pay for their law breaking. Because blood is the source of life, God's plan for payment involved the spilling of blood. . . .
>
> Animals were to be sacrificed as payment for sin. Though the curse could not be broken by these sacrifices, the shed blood of an

animal would provide temporary cover from God's punishment of their sin.[1]

This kind of approach is mainstream. Although not all interpreters would offer this specific answer, it's common for discussions of Leviticus to explain why God had a very good reason for commanding the Israelites to offer sacrifices. But I'm convinced that these are answers to the wrong question. Yes, God commands sacrifice in Leviticus—but sacrifice was already happening before God gave these commands. Up to that point, most sacrifices described in scripture were not commanded by God. Even the opening chapters of Leviticus *assume* sacrifice rather than command it: "When any of you bring an offering of livestock to the LORD, . . ."[2] In other words, the story scripture tells is one in which sacrifice *wasn't God's idea in the first place*; the laws in Leviticus just acknowledge and regulate what the Israelites were already doing.

Let's walk through the examples. The first recorded sacrifices are the ones brought by Cain and Abel;[3] the Hebrew term for their offering is *minchah*, which has the more general meaning of "gift" or "offering" but can also be used for formal sacrifices, especially of grain.[4] There's no hint that God asked for these offerings. Similarly, God didn't ask for sacrifices from Noah and didn't ask Abram to build altars, but they did so anyway.[5]

The first story where it looks like God commanded someone to offer a sacrifice comes in Genesis 15. God makes a covenant with Abram, promising to give the land of Canaan to his descendants. He asks Abram to bring several animals; Abram cuts them in two, and God sends a vision of a smoking pot and a torch to pass between the pieces. The text doesn't explicitly call this a sacrifice, and it's not clear whether all this happened on an altar or on the ground, but there's at least a strong family resemblance to other sacrificial rituals. (Interestingly, we don't see God telling Abram to cut the animals in two; I'm not sure whether we're supposed to infer that he did and it's not mentioned, or that Abram just knew what to do.)

The whole episode seems to be a unique event; there's no suggestion that God told Abram to keep offering sacrifices on a regular basis. Nor do we read any instructions about regular sacrifices in Genesis 22, when God

1. *Life Book*, 14.
2. Lev 1:2.
3. Gen 4:3–5.
4. Lev 2.
5. Gen 8:20; 12:7–8; 13:18.

commands Abraham to offer his son Isaac as a burnt offering (an *'olah*). After God stops Abraham at the last moment, Abraham sees a ram caught in the bushes and offers that in his place. One reading of this story is that God is saying child sacrifice is unacceptable and animals should be offered instead. This interpretation is reasonable enough, but notice that it makes sense only if sacrifice (of some kind) was something people were *already* doing, without being commanded to do so by God.

For the rest of Genesis, we see Isaac and his son Jacob building altars[6] and offering sacrifices,[7] apparently of their own accord. There's one occasion when Jacob builds an altar in response to a direct command from God.[8] As with Abram in Genesis 15, God doesn't tell Jacob to offer sacrifices on the altar, although it's not much of a stretch to suppose that Jacob should have understood that sacrifices were implied. (Really, what else was he supposed to do with an altar? We do have stories of nonsacrificial altars,[9] but not many.) And here, in one of the few instances where God gives a direct command to one of the patriarchs about sacrificial worship, the text doesn't explicitly record that Jacob actually offered any sacrifices there! Maybe we're supposed to infer that he did, but it's interesting that the story treats the actual sacrifices—if they even happened—as unimportant. At any rate, the overall picture suggests that most sacrifices were a matter of human initiative. God lets human beings worship him through sacrifice, but it's not the only way he relates to people, or even the most important one.

After Jacob's family travels to Egypt and their descendants are enslaved, references to sacrifice drop out—unsurprisingly, since it's hard to imagine the Israelites having the resources for expensive animal sacrifice after four hundred years of slavery. But when Moses confronts Pharaoh to demand their freedom, he explains, "[L]et us go a three days' journey into the wilderness to sacrifice to the LORD our God,"[10] as though sacrifice is a perfectly normal thing to do. Surely this implies that sacrifice was a common practice among the Israelites' neighbors.

If sacrifice was widespread outside of Israel, then there ought to be archaeological evidence for it. And that's exactly what we have; temples and texts from the Ancient Near East make it abundantly clear that sacrifice was

---

6. Gen 26:25; 33:20.
7. Gen 31:54–55; 46:1.
8. Gen 35:1–14.
9. Josh 22:10–29.
10. Exod 5:3.

everywhere, for thousands of years. We'll see plenty of examples of non-Israelite rituals in the next few chapters. But the point I want to make here is that this understanding of sacrifice, as a widespread cultural practice that long predates the Israelites, isn't an esoteric idea accessible only to people with degrees in archaeology. It's the story scripture itself tells. When we read scripture closely, we don't find a demanding God who requires sacrifices from reluctant humans. Instead, we discover a story in which humans start offering sacrifices before God ever says a word about the subject.

To say that sacrifice was our idea, not God's, is actually a very old suggestion. The twelfth-century Jewish philosopher Maimonides develops this line of reasoning at length in his *Guide for the Perplexed*.[11] He argues that God never intended for humans to offer sacrifices, but that the Israelites were so used to the practice that it would have been asking too much to command them not to. So, instead, God put limits on sacrifice, severely restricting the places where it could be done—unlike prayer, which God didn't restrict at all. Maimonides compares the way God dealt with sacrifice to his leading the Israelites from Egypt to Canaan on a roundabout route;[12] it was a temporary accommodation to what the people were ready for.

Maimonides isn't alone. Some early Christian writers made the same argument,[13] and there are plenty of modern interpreters who agree, both Jewish[14] and Christian.[15] At this point, there are a couple of interpretive paths we could take. One is to rail against those foolish Jews who needed something as barbaric as sacrifice to keep them in line. Shamefully (but unsurprisingly), some Christians have done exactly that; John Chrysostom, preaching in the fourth century, gives us an excellent specimen:

> [God] saw the Jews choking with their mad yearning for sacrifices. He saw that they were ready to go over to idols if they were deprived of sacrifices, I should say, he saw that they were not only ready to go over, but that they had already done so. So he let them have their sacrifices.... After they kept the festival in honor of the evil demons [the golden calf], God yielded and permitted

---

11. Maimonides, *Guide* 3.32.
12. Exod 13:17–18.
13. Poorthuis, "Sacrifice as Concession," 170–91; Theodoret, *Questions* 1.1.
14. Hertz, *Pentateuch and Haftorahs*, 410.
15. Bell, "Blood, Guts, & Fire;" Chingota, "Leviticus," 134.

sacrifices. What he all but said was this: "You are all eager and avid for sacrifices. If sacrifice you must, then sacrifice to me."[16]

That way lies anti-Semitism, of which Chrysostom himself—and his subsequent interpreters—is a prime example.

A much better path is to acknowledge that sacrifice has been deeply meaningful in many, many cultures—not just in Judaism!—and to ask what we can learn from it. The mere fact that people spontaneously choose to worship God in some way, without a direct commandment first, doesn't *by itself* mean that the practice has no value and ought to be discarded as soon as possible. You could tell exactly the same story about music that I've told here about sacrifice: scripture describes people singing praise to God without, apparently, any prior commandment to do so.[17] Music is presented approvingly throughout scripture, but there's nothing even close to a commandment to sing until long after it was well established.[18] (Yes, God teaches Moses a song in Deuteronomy 31–32, but its explicit purpose is to instruct the Israelites; there's no hint that they should be using it, or anything else, in worship.) And music is an extremely common part of religious practice across cultures. For whatever reason, singing is a spontaneous human activity; but it's one that God is happy to include in worship.

The larger point I want to make isn't that animal sacrifice was basically a human idea, although in my opinion that really is the story scripture tells. Rather, my point is that the Old Testament does *not* describe a world where the Israelites offered sacrifices reluctantly and only because God forced them to do so. Even if we assume that God must have told Adam and Eve to sacrifice and Genesis simply doesn't record it (which some interpreters have done[19])—well, it strains credulity to suppose that generation after generation would have kept doing this without continued instruction from God, *unless sacrifice was something people wanted to do anyway*. Either way, we come to the same conclusion: the laws about sacrifice in Leviticus have a context, and that context is a world where sacrifice is normal, expected, and valued.

16. John Chrysostom, *Adv. Jud.* 4.6.5.
17. Exod 15:1–21; Judg 5:1–41; 2 Sam 6:5.
18. Isa 12:5–6; Jer 31:7; Eph 5:19; Col 3:16.
19. Assohoto and Ngewa, "Genesis," 17; Landry, *Light in the Shadows*, 89; Levy, *Tabernacle*, 92.

Enthusiasm for sacrifice in the Old Testament

If we read the narrative of scripture closely, by the time we get to Leviticus we see that people have been offering sacrifices for a long time. As we continue the story after Leviticus, a similar theme emerges. We know very little about everyday religious practice in ancient Israel, but almost every single reference to sacrifice outside of the Pentateuch paints a picture of people offering sacrifices willingly, even enthusiastically. (Sometimes it seems like sacrifice is just about the only part of the law that was actually followed!)

This theme is clearest in the passages that criticize sacrifice; the problem is almost never that people are neglecting sacrifice, but rather that they're doing it wrong or instead of something more important. The sons of Eli the priest officiate at sacrifices and take meat they aren't entitled to.[20] Saul presumptuously offers sacrifices himself instead of waiting for Samuel to officiate.[21] After Solomon builds the temple in Jerusalem, the author of 1 and 2 Kings criticizes the people for offering sacrifices on the "high places" or at other sanctuaries instead of at the Jerusalem temple.[22]

The prophets have a lot to say about sacrifice, little of it good. Their recurring theme is that the people are offering sacrifices but acting wickedly; God rejects such empty religious rituals. Isaiah develops this subject at length:

> When you come to appear before me,
>   who asked this from your hand?
>   Trample my courts no more;
> bringing offerings is futile;
>   incense is an abomination to me.
> New moon and sabbath and calling of convocation—
>   I cannot endure solemn assemblies with iniquity.
> Your new moons and your appointed festivals
>   my soul hates;
> they have become a burden to me,
>   I am weary of bearing them.
> When you stretch out your hands,
>   I will hide my eyes from you;
> even though you make many prayers,
>   I will not listen;
>   your hands are full of blood.

---

20. 1 Sam 2:12–17.
21. 1 Sam 13:8–14.
22. 1 Kgs 12:28–33; 22:43; 2 Kgs 12:3; 14:4; 15:4, 35; 16:4; 21:3–5.

> Wash yourselves; make yourselves clean;
> > remove the evil of your doings
> > from before my eyes;
> cease to do evil,
> > learn to do good;
> seek justice,
> > rescue the oppressed,
> defend the orphan,
> > plead for the widow.[23]

Similarly, Amos observes that the Israelites love to sacrifice. God is no more impressed by Amos's contemporaries than he is by Isaiah's:

> Come to Bethel—and transgress;
> > to Gilgal—and multiply transgression;
> bring your sacrifices every morning,
> > your tithes every three days;
> bring a thank offering of leavened bread,
> > and proclaim freewill offerings, publish them;
> for so you love to do, O people of Israel![24]

> I hate, I despise your festivals,
> > and I take no delight in your solemn assemblies.
> Even though you offer me your burnt offerings [*'olot*] and grain offerings,
> > I will not accept them;
> and the offerings of well-being [*shelem*] of your fatted animals
> > I will not look upon.
> Take away from me the noise of your songs;
> > I will not listen to the melody of your harps.
> But let justice roll down like waters,
> > and righteousness like an ever-flowing stream.[25]

Passages like these have been used to argue that sacrifice is worthless; after all, God seems to be rejecting the practice in pretty strong terms. But in context, it's clear that the problem is not sacrifice itself, but rather empty religion devoid of ethics. Isaiah also mentions prayer and Amos mentions singing; surely God isn't rejecting those practices too! What he objects to is worship accompanied by injustice. At any rate, the relevant point here is

---

23. Isa 1:12–17.
24. Amos 4:4–5.
25. Amos 5:21–24.

that the prophets don't criticize people for not sacrificing enough; if anything, they're sacrificing too much.

And then, of course, there's the abundant evidence that the Israelites sacrificed to other gods. The Old Testament tells of people offering sacrifices to Baal and other neighboring gods;[26] Jeremiah criticizes his contemporaries for making offerings to "the queen of heaven."[27] That's how enthusiastic people were about sacrifice: not only did they make plenty of sacrifices to the Lord (even while ignoring him in many other ways), but they made *extra* sacrifices to other gods. And it isn't just that some people wanted to replace their own onerous sacrifices with something more fun that the priests of Baal or another god were doing. Some of that happened too—for example, the kings Hezekiah and Josiah had to repair the temple, which had apparently been neglected[28]—but it's clear that at various times there was side-by-side worship of multiple gods, including the Lord. Ezekiel explicitly condemns worshippers who sacrifice to idols (probably in the valley of Hinnom, a site in Jerusalem notorious for child sacrifice[29]) and then go up to the temple to worship God *on the same day.*[30]

The psalms give us another view of this positive regard for sacrifice. The psalms don't hold back from expressing grief, anger, or despair, even towards God: "How long, O Lord? Will you forget me forever? How long will you hide your face from me?"[31] Nor do they pull their punches on religious practices; Psalm 50 offers a criticism of overzealous sacrifice that sounds very much like the prophets. What we *don't* see in the psalms is any complaint that sacrifice is a burden, something like this:

> O Lord, why do you command so many sacrifices?
>   I am weary of bringing them.
> I dread coming to your temple;
>   when I bring a sin offering, I am overwhelmed with sorrow.

We don't even see the psalmists criticizing other people (or their past selves) for feeling this way:

> O Lord, in my youth I was foolish;

26. 1 Kgs 16:32; 18:26; Jer 11:13; Ezek 6:13; 20:28; Hos 11:2.
27. Jer 7:18; 44:25.
28. 2 Chr 29:3–36; 34:8–12.
29. Jer 19:1–7.
30. Ezek 23:38–39.
31. Ps 13:1.

> I despised your sacrifices;
>> I said, "What use are they?"
> But then I went to your temple and learned wisdom;
>> I was instructed at your altar.
> Now I bring burnt offerings with joy;
>> I bring sin offerings with a glad heart.

I see no reason psalms like these couldn't have been included in scripture; the feelings they express are no more shocking than the psalms we actually have! But they simply don't exist. Instead, the psalmists regularly look forward to offering sacrifices.[32] Occasionally a psalmist describes some other activity as better than sacrifice: "Sacrifice and offering you do not desire, . . . I delight to do your will, O my God; your law is within my heart."[33] "For you have no delight in sacrifice; if I were to give a burnt offering, you would not be pleased. The sacrifice acceptable to God is a broken spirit; a broken and contrite heart, O God, you will not despise."[34] Notice the difference: the psalmists aren't saying "I don't want to sacrifice" or "all sacrifice is bad;" they're saying that, in this situation, God wants something else. In fact, these psalms don't sound at all out of place next to twentieth-century Christian worship songs: "I'll bring you more than a song, for a song in itself is not what you have required."[35] The psalmists aren't rejecting sacrifice any more than Matt Redman is rejecting worship music (his sentiment is captured, after all, in a song!).

Even some of the laws in Leviticus seem to assume that sacrifice is something people actually enjoy, at least some of the time. The regulations for voluntary sacrifices[36] make no sense if sacrifice is something you do only when you're required to. (Imagine if the IRS set up rules for how to pay extra taxes beyond what you legally owe, just because you feel like it. Those rules would be pointless; no one would use them.) In Leviticus 26, God describes in graphic terms what will happen if the Israelites fail to keep the law; one of the many grim consequences is that "I will . . . make your sanctuaries desolate, and I will not smell your pleasing [sacrificial] odors."[37] Unless sacrifices were viewed as a positive thing, it's hard to see how this

---

32. Pss 27:6; 43:4; 54:6; 56:12; 66:13–15; 116:17.
33. Ps 40:6a, 8.
34. Ps 51:16–17.
35. Redman, "Heart of Worship."
36. Lev 7:11–18; 22:17–30.
37. Lev 26:31.

counts as a punishment. "Son, if you don't keep your grades up, I will forbid you from taking out the garbage!"

Love for sacrifice wasn't exceptionless. In addition to the periodic neglect of the temple noted above, there are two other passages that suggest that sacrifice was sometimes experienced as something negative. One passage in Isaiah describes people who aren't bringing sacrifices;[38] another in Malachi criticizes the sacrifice of defective animals.[39] Certainly, it's not surprising that sacrifice would be seen as a burden in particular times and particular places; the same thing can happen with any religious practice. (Surely no one would argue that Christian celebration of the Lord's supper is supposed to be burdensome, but that doesn't mean no Christian has ever felt that way about it.) Examples like these are in the minority, though; overwhelmingly, the story of sacrifice in the Old Testament is the story of a practice that faithful worshippers of God found meaningful and joyous. A theology in which sacrifice was a perpetual guilt trip, a constant reminder of sin that people got rid of as soon as they could, simply doesn't do justice to scripture.

Attraction of Judaism in the Second Temple period

The Old Testament consistently portrays sacrifice as a normal part of religious practice—and as something that, for ordinary people, was far more often a source of joy than a burden. When we come to the Second Temple period, and particularly to the time of Jesus, both scripture and extra-biblical sources paint a remarkably similar picture.

Overall, it's clear that the temple—which had many functions but was centered around sacrifice—was revered and respected.[40] Those who criticized the temple almost always objected to how the priests in charge were running things at the moment, not to the institution of sacrifice itself. Even the Qumran sectarians, who thought the temple was so corrupted that they had to go off and build their own community in the desert (and whose library is now known to us as the Dead Sea Scrolls), looked forward to the day when correct temple worship would be restored, including proper animal sacrifice.[41]

38. Isa 43:23–24.
39. Mal 1:6–14.
40. Sanders, *Judaism*, 76–80.
41. Klawans, *Symbolism and Supersessionism*, 145–74.

Judaism wasn't unique in this regard. Josephus, who wrote for a Gentile audience, defended *how* Jews offered sacrifices but not *that* they offered sacrifices. Philo of Alexandria, influenced by Greek philosophy, wrote extensively about how sacrifices symbolized various spiritual truths (more on this in chapter 5). But even he insisted that literal observance of the law, including literal sacrifice, was vital too.[42] Philo even retells the story of the Passover in a remarkable way: the Israelites sacrificed lambs, not to escape the last plague that fell on the Egyptians, but because they were so overjoyed at their freedom that they started sacrificing right away, without even waiting for official priests to be appointed.[43] This story is strikingly different from the one told in Exodus 11–13; what's interesting for our purposes here is that Philo expects it to make sense for his readers: of course sacrifice is a beautiful and joyful thing to do, and it's only natural that the Israelites would start as soon as they got the chance.

In fact, for Gentiles who were attracted to Judaism, the most common obstacle to full conversion (especially for men) seems to have been circumcision,[44] not sacrifice. And Gentiles observing at least part of Jewish law, to a greater or lesser extent, weren't uncommon. Josephus tells of Helena and Izates, a queen and king (mother and son) of Adiabene who converted to Judaism, and even describes a journey that Helena voluntarily made to Jerusalem in order to worship at the temple and offer sacrifices.[45] He also reports that the perpetrators of a massacre in Damascus had to be careful because there was so much pro-Jewish sentiment in the city:

> Meanwhile the Damascenes, once they learned about the loss of the Romans, were eager to do away with the Judeans among themselves. On the one hand, insofar as they were holding them in the gymnasium . . . they supposed that the project would be easy; on the other hand, they had come to be worried about their own wives, who had all—but for a few—been attracted by the Judean worship. Consequently, the biggest struggle for them was escaping [their wives'] notice.[46]

---

42. Philo, *Migr.* 89–93.
43. Philo, *Spec.* 2.145–46.
44. Ferguson, *Backgrounds*, 550.
45. Josephus, *A.J.* 20.2.
46. Josephus, *B.J.* 2.20.2 (Mason).

(Tragically, the men managed to murder thousands of Jews anyway.) The New Testament, too, regularly mentions "God-fearing" Gentiles who were sympathetic to Judaism.[47]

The gospels describe Jesus teaching and healing in the temple,[48] and the book of Acts describes the disciples continuing to meet there after Jesus' death[49] and Paul traveling there for the express purpose of offering a sacrifice.[50] There's no explicit story of Jesus offering a sacrifice, but most likely he and his disciples would have done so when they celebrated Passover. In addition, as discussed in chapter 1, his teaching on anger assumed that his disciples would continue to sacrifice,[51] and he instructed healed lepers to offer sacrifices for purification.[52] Jesus never told his disciples to stop sacrificing, and his teaching was never "Good news! You don't have to sacrifice anymore." So, even though Christians did eventually conclude that Jesus' death made sacrifices unnecessary, Jesus himself didn't make getting rid of sacrifice a top priority.

It was only a few decades after Jesus' death that the Romans destroyed the Jerusalem temple, rendering the issue of sacrifices practically (if not theoretically) moot: there was nowhere to offer them anyway. But the boundary between Jews and Christians remained highly porous for a long time; when John Chrysostom blasted Jews for their supposed addiction to sacrifices, he was trying to convince members of his own congregation that they should stop going to synagogues (in addition to church!) and celebrating Jewish festivals.[53]

When we set out to understand sacrifice and other ritual practices of the Old Testament, our conclusions will be shaped by the larger story we tell about them. One common story among Christians is that these laws were pretty terrible; God intended them to be a burden, people hated them, and when Jesus came along Christians abandoned them as soon as possible. I've argued in these first two chapters that this story is wrong: it's inconsistent

---

47. Luke 7:2–5; John 12:20–21; Acts 10:1–2; 16:14; 18:7.

48. Matt 21:14, 23; 26:55; Mark 11:27; 12:35; 14:49; Luke 19:47; 20:1; 21:37–38; 22:53; John 7:14; 8:2, 20; 10:23; 18:20.

49. Acts 2:46; 3:1; 5:12–21, 42.

50. Acts 21:17–26.

51. Matt 5:23–24.

52. Matt 8:2–4 // Mark 1:40–44 // Luke 5:12–14; Luke 17:12–14.

53. Fonrobert, "Judaizers," 637–40.

with the story scripture *actually* tells, and it doesn't fit with what we know about Second Temple Judaism.

A better story is that these practices were somehow fundamentally *good*—and, perhaps just as important, that they were generally experienced that way. This doesn't mean that we should revive animal sacrifice today (just to be clear, I'm not in favor of this). Nor does it mean Christians can't claim that Jesus makes sacrifice obsolete; one practice can still be good even if something else is better. And it doesn't mean that we can't criticize sacrifice; it's perfectly legitimate to point out the ethical issues involved in terms of how we treat animals. What it *does* mean is that we need to start from a place of respect and curiosity: Why do so many people, across cultures and throughout time, find these rituals meaningful? How do they help humans encounter God? What can we learn from them about how God relates to his people? With these questions in hand, we're ready to take a closer look at the sacrificial regulations themselves.

3

WHAT SACRIFICE IS NOT

SUPPOSE I TELL YOU that Bob gave flowers to Jane. In contemporary western culture, this is a perfectly ordinary thing to do—giving flowers is a traditional act in a way that, say, giving toner cartridges isn't. You understand that Bob is expressing something more than "here are some dying plants."

But even though giving flowers is a conventional social action, it doesn't have just one meaning. If you know that Bob gave Jane flowers but you don't know anything more about the circumstances, you can imagine all sorts of reasons for the gift. Bob could be asking Jane on a date. He could be congratulating her on the opening night of her play. He could be celebrating a birthday or an anniversary. He could be saying "I'm sorry" or "thank you" or "I love you."

John Goldingay points out that sacrifice in the ancient world was a lot like giving flowers in ours.[1] It was a conventional social action, perfectly ordinary and with accepted cultural meanings. But it didn't have just one meaning; it could have several, depending on the context (or even within the same ritual!). One thing I especially like about this analogy is how closely the occasions for sacrifice in the Old Testament match occasions for giving flowers today. Sacrifices were used to make a covenant (that is, to begin a relationship), to thank God for some specific action ("thank you" or "congratulations"), to celebrate an annual festival ("happy anniversary"), to repair a relationship broken by sin ("I'm sorry"), or just to praise God ("I love you").

---

1. Goldingay, "Old Testament Sacrifice," 1–20.

This perspective is a helpful corrective to the attempt, popular in many circles, to try to discern The One Thing That Sacrifice Is All About. In this way of thinking, there's a fundamental Something, common to all sacrifices, that gives them their meaning. Even if some sacrificial ritual seems to be unrelated to the One Thing, if you squint hard enough you'll see that it's *really* about the One Thing after all. And so all sacrifices are fundamentally about reenacting a hunting ritual, or appeasing an angry deity, or redirecting communal violence, or whatever your favorite theory is. Peel back the layers of the onion, and eventually you'll reach the true center.

I prefer to think of sacrifice, not as an onion, but as a bulb of garlic. Garlic doesn't have one center, but many. Each clove has a papery outer layer that you can remove to get to the good stuff inside, but there's no One Clove That Explains All the Others. Some cloves are larger than others, some are more central than others, but none are independent; each clove's shape is affected by its neighbors, so that all the cloves nestle together tightly to form one whole bulb.

We'll spend the next three chapters looking at some of the "cloves" of sacrifice in the Old Testament. Chapter 4 explores sacrifices as they relate to sin; chapter 5 describes the many non-sin-related functions of sacrifice. This chapter starts by looking at some meanings sacrifice did *not* have in the Old Testament, although those meanings were present in neighboring cultures. (I use "neighboring" in an extremely loose sense; we'll see examples of ideas and rituals from communities that may have been separated by thousands of miles and thousands of years. The point is not that the Israelites heard some ideas directly from the Greeks, or vice versa—we're limited by which ancient documents have survived into modern times, which aren't necessarily those of the Israelites' closest neighbors—but that we can use ancient texts to get an idea of how some ancient people thought about the world and the gods.) God may have used common ideas about sacrifice to shape Israel's worship, but there were certain ideas that he emphatically rejected.

Food for God

One widespread belief about sacrifice in the ancient world was that it provided food for the gods. Some descriptions, such as the following Akkadian ritual text, are quite explicit that the sacrificed animals constitute a meal.

> For the main meal of the evening, the regular offering to the deities Anu and Antu and the household gods of the temples, throughout

the year: four fat, clean rams which have been fed barley for two years; one fat, milk-fed *kalū*-ram of the regular offering; five other rams which, unlike the previously mentioned, have not been fed barley; and ten . . . birds.[2]

If you're concerned that this seems a bit protein-heavy, not to worry: feeding the gods wasn't limited to animal sacrifice; plenty of gods got a balanced diet.

> Upon seven large golden trays, you shall present water for washing hands to the planets Jupiter, Venus, Mercury, Saturn, Mars, the moon, and the sun, as soon as they appear. Then you shall set the tray and serve bull meat, ram meat, and fowl. You shall also serve prime beer together with pressed wine. You shall heap up all types of garden produce. You shall sprinkle cedar resin and *mashatu*-flour upon seven golden censers, and then you shall make a libation of pressed wine from a golden libation vessel.[3]

Some cultures, although not necessarily all, thought that the gods depend on humans to feed and sustain them. Regardless of how literally this was meant, the image was one where priests are servants waiting at their master's table; they can earn the master's favor by doing their job well, but if they fail in their duties, the master will be rightfully angry.

> When the servant stands before his master, he is washed and he has clothed himself in clean clothes. He gives his master either to eat or to drink. Since this man's master eats and drinks, in his spirit he is relaxed. He becomes indebted to him. But if, at some point, the servant is negligent, is his master not irritated? Is the spirit of the god somehow different?[4]

At first glance, there might appear to be some hints of this idea in the Old Testament. One of the pieces of furniture inside the sanctuary was a table where the priests put twelve fresh loaves of bread every week: the "bread of the presence."[5] Moreover, some translations refer to certain sacrifices as "food offerings" (e.g., Lev 1:9 in the 2011 NIV). On this second point, the Hebrew word translated "food offering" (*'ishsheh*) has traditionally been translated "offering by fire" (as in the NRSV and the 1984 NIV),

---

2. "Akkadian Rituals," trans. A. Sachs, *ANET*, 344.
3. "Akkadian Rituals," trans. A. Sachs, *ANET*, 338.
4. Mouton, "Animal Sacrifice," 251.
5. Exod 25:23–30; Lev 24:5–7; 1 Sam 21:6.

because *'ishsheh* appears to be related to *'esh*, "fire." But some scholars have proposed that *'ishsheh* does *not* mean "fire," pointing out that related languages have a similar word that means "gift."[6] "Gift" makes better sense in context; some of the offerings described as *'ishsheh*, including the bread of the presence,[7] aren't burned at all! The translation "food offering," or "food gift," is supposed to represent the fact that parts of these *'ishsheh* offerings often (although not always) provide food *for the priests*—not for God. The upshot of all this is that although we see references to "food" in some English translations, that connotation isn't necessarily present in the Hebrew.

Not only do the rituals around sacrifice and the sanctuary not encourage an interpretation of sacrifice as food, but the Old Testament explicitly *discourages* this interpretation. Psalm 50 describes God rejecting this idea in no uncertain terms:

> I will not accept a bull from your house,
>   or goats from your folds.
> For every wild animal of the forest is mine,
>   the cattle on a thousand hills.
> I know all the birds of the air,
>   and all that moves in the field is mine.
> If I were hungry, I would not tell you,
>   for the world and all that is in it is mine.
> Do I eat the flesh of bulls,
>   or drink the blood of goats?[8]

The apocryphal account of "Bel and the Dragon" makes the same point. This pair of short stories is appended to the book of Daniel in some Greek versions; it's accepted as scripture by the Catholic and Orthodox churches, although not by Protestants or in Judaism. The first story tells how Daniel confronts a pagan king who insists that the god Bel is real; who else could be eating all the food offered to Bel's statue? Daniel secretly spreads ashes on the floor of the temple; the next morning, the ashes reveal the footprints of the priests who have been sneaking in to eat the food at night, thus proving that the idol isn't a god after all.

This story is entertaining; we get to watch our hero Daniel emerge victorious from yet another showdown with foreign oppressors. And it

---

6. Milgrom, *Leviticus 1–16*, 161–62.
7. Lev 24:7.
8. Ps 50:9–13.

teaches an important theological lesson about the superiority of the Lord to so-called gods who need to be sustained by human offerings. But, in reality, it's unlikely that everyone in the ancient world thought the gods literally ate the food that was offered to them. We can give people in ancient times more credit than that; it was probably no secret that the priests were the ones who ate most of the food, and that food offerings were symbolic. Nevertheless, the Old Testament makes clear that God rejects even a symbolic understanding of sacrifice as food for himself. Sacrifice means many things, but not this.

Bribery

In a world where sacrifice means giving something valuable to the gods, it's not a large step to the idea that sacrifice is—to put it crudely—a form of bribery. I give the gods food, or valuable animals, and in exchange I expect them to give me what I ask for: health, success in battle, a good harvest. And in fact it's not hard to find people making a direct connection between sacrifice and favors from the gods. Consider the story of the archery contest in the *Iliad*, where the god Apollo rewards those who sacrifice and punishes those who don't:

> And at once
> [Teucer] fired an arrow with power—but he forgot to promise to King
> Apollo the glorious sacrifice of new-born sheep, and so he
> missed the bird. Apollo begrudged him the shot, but he hit
> the cord beside the bird's foot where the bird was tied to the pole.
> The bitter arrow went straight through the cord, and the dove flew
> to the heavens while the cord hung loose toward the ground.
> All the Achaeans shouted aloud.
> But Meriones speedily grabbed
> the bow from Teucer's hand—he had long held an arrow
> while Teucer took his shot. At once he vowed to Apollo,
> who works from a long way off, to offer a glorious sacrifice
> from his new-born lambs. He saw the timid dove high
> beneath the clouds. There, as she circled around, he hit
> her in the middle beneath the wing.[9]

It's possible to read this as a story in which Meriones's promise is purely self-serving, and Apollo is a corrupt judge who rewards whoever gives him

---

9. Homer, *Il.* 23.829–42.

the best bribe. Other accounts in the *Iliad* could be read the same way; for example, Zeus says that Hector, a prince of Troy, "was dearest to the gods. . . . [H]e never failed of acceptable gifts. Never did my altar lack in the equal feast, or in the drink-offering, or in the smoke of sacrifice."[10]

But before we conclude that ancient worshippers had a purely transactional relationship with the gods, let's think back to the flower analogy. Suppose Jane goes on two dates, one with Bob and one with Sam; Bob brings flowers, but Sam doesn't. If Jane decides that she likes Bob better because he brought her flowers, does that mean Bob was bribing Jane? Well, maybe, but not necessarily. Sure, Jane could be a gold-digger who hopes Bob will bring her expensive gifts, and Bob could be a cad who thinks he can buy someone's affection. But Jane could make a similar judgment even without mercenary motives; maybe Bob's flowers aren't a bribe, but rather a symbol of his commitment to her and to their relationship.

Similarly, these ancient stories *could* indicate a transactional view of sacrifice, but they don't *have* to. In a Greek context, Lucian, quoted in chapter 1, was one of many writers who criticized the idea that the gods could be bought; ancient thinkers were perfectly capable of seeing the problematic moral implications of an economic model of sacrifice. For many ordinary worshippers, the exchange of offerings and divine favors was perhaps more like an ongoing exchange of gifts between friends, albeit highly unequal ones. Especially noteworthy for Christians is that this relationship was characterized by a mutual exchange of *charis*, "grace"![11]

What's interesting about the Old Testament is that the reciprocal logic of sacrifice—whether in a crude transactional sense or in a rich relational sense—is only hinted at. We have only a handful of stories of sacrifices that are explicitly connected to God doing something for the offerer, and in many cases *God* is the one who takes the initiative. God instructs Abram to bring a sacrifice to seal a covenant[12] and David to build an altar to stop a plague,[13] but in both cases God's action is something he has *already decided to do*.[14] Essentially, the sacrifice only represents God's decision after the fact. We could say something similar about God's promise after Abraham shows

---

10. Homer, *Il.* 24.68–71.
11. Parker, "Pleasing Thighs," 105–25.
12. Gen 15:7–21.
13. 2 Sam 24:18.
14. 2 Sam 24:16.

WHAT SACRIFICE IS NOT

that he's willing to sacrifice Isaac;[15] he had *already* promised to multiply Abraham's descendants and bless all people through them.[16] (Similarly, Jacob's promise to give a tenth of all his possessions to God comes *after* God's unconditional promise to bless him and his descendants.[17]) The context of God's command to the returned exiles to "test me"[18] is more about tithes than about sacrifices, and is presented as a reassurance that their limited resources won't be overburdened by giving God his due rather than an explanation that this is how sacrifice usually works.

Humans occasionally take the initiative too; Absalom claims to have made a vow that he would sacrifice to God in Hebron if God brought him back to Jerusalem.[19] (Whether Absalom really did make such a vow, or whether the whole thing was a ruse to arrange a coup, is another question.) Jephthah promises to offer a sacrifice if God gives him victory in battle, although since he ends up offering his own daughter the story is hardly presented as a worthy example to imitate.[20] Noah doesn't explicitly ask for anything in return when he offers a sacrifice, but the text hints that God responds nevertheless.[21] Hannah's promise that if God gives her a son she will dedicate him to the Lord illustrates that reciprocity wasn't confined to the sacrificial system.[22]

Perhaps the best narrative contrast is between Saul and David. King Saul regularly sacrifices in connection with military campaigns, but we read about God rejecting those sacrifices because Saul is disobeying other commands.[23] By contrast, we don't have any stories of king David sacrificing to ask for a military victory, and yet God is with him and gives him success wherever he goes. At least as far as ad-hoc sacrifices go, God is portrayed as a low-maintenance spouse: he's happy to receive them, but he doesn't demand them. What he *does* demand is faithfulness to the covenant; he's no more impressed by a sacrifice from an unfaithful partner than a spouse would be by flowers. This is what the author of Ecclesiastes is getting at:

15. Gen 22:15–18.
16. Gen 12:1–3.
17. Gen 28:13–22.
18. Mal 3:8–11.
19. 2 Sam 15:7–12.
20. Judg 11:30–39.
21. Gen 8:20–21.
22. 1 Sam 1:11.
23. 1 Sam 13:8–14; 15:13–23.

"When you make a vow to God, do not delay in fulfilling it; for he has no pleasure in fools. Fulfill what you vow. It is better that you should not vow than that you should vow and not fulfill it."[24]

Besides stories, if we're looking for people asking God for specific acts of favor, the place to go is the book of Psalms, which has no shortage of cries for help. And yes, some psalms do talk about offering a sacrifice as thanks for God's deliverance:

> I will come into your house with burnt offerings [*'olot*];
>   I will pay you my vows,
> those that my lips uttered
>   and my mouth promised when I was in trouble.
> I will offer to you burnt offerings [*'olot*] of fatlings,
>   with the smoke of the sacrifice of rams;
> I will make an offering of bulls and goats.[25]

Although they do exist, psalms like this aren't terribly common. Out of 150 psalms, I count only nine that describe a sacrifice or vows in exchange for God's help,[26] plus four more that mention worshipping at the temple or an altar (which plausibly could involve sacrifice).[27] A much stronger theme in the psalms is that the psalmist will publicly tell the story of what God has done for him.[28] In fact, sometimes the point of a sacrifice seems to be, not that it repays God in itself, but that it gives the worshipper the chance to praise God in a public setting. Psalm 66, just quoted, continues with exactly this idea:

> Come and hear, all you who fear God,
>   and I will tell what he has done for me.
> I cried aloud to him,
>   and he was extolled with my tongue.
> If I had cherished iniquity in my heart,
>   the Lord would not have listened.[29]

---

24. Eccl 5:4–5.
25. Ps 66:13–15.
26. Pss 20, 22, 27, 54, 56, 61, 66, 107, 116.
27. Pss 5, 26, 43, 118.
28. Pss 6, 9, 30, 35, 40, 52, 57, 69, 71, 102, 109.
29. Ps 66:16–18.

Some psalms explicitly say that this kind of praise is more important than sacrifice.[30]

The last verse just quoted from Psalm 66 illustrates yet another feature of the psalms. In the *Iliad*, the priest Chryses prays to Apollo to help him, on the grounds that Chryses has offered many sacrifices to Apollo.[31] This kind of appeal to someone's past sacrifices is extremely rare in the psalms; I can find only one example.[32] Much more common is an appeal to the psalmist's past ethical deeds—not offering sacrifices that must now be repaid, but doing good and avoiding evil.[33] It's the difference between "Think of how often I bring you flowers" and "Remember how I treat you with respect, and help your mother when she's sick, and always keep my promises." The former is fine, as far as it goes, but the latter really gets to the heart of the relationship.

Finally, although plenty of psalms ask for help because of something the *psalmist* has done, we shouldn't lose sight of the fact that the vast majority of laments (if they give a reason at all) ground their request for help in *God's* nature: his commitment to justice and to his people.[34] The dominant theme of the psalms is that God is eager to help his people, not because of who they are, but because of who he is.

To sum up: the idea that sacrifice is a gift to God, with the expectation that God will grant favors in return, is marginal at best in the Old Testament. And sacrifice as a bribe has no support whatsoever in scripture. In this sense, the Israelites may not have been so very different from their neighbors. Did some individuals think they could buy blessings with sacrifices? Certainly, but that doesn't mean this is what God intended. (And before we start feeling superior to those foolish ancients with their primitive ideas of what God is like, look around at the popularity of the prosperity gospel today.) Sacrifices may sometimes be like gifts, but only within the context of God's relationship with his people.

---

30. Pss 40:6–10; 69:30–31.
31. Homer, *Il.* 1.35–45.
32. Ps 20.
33. Pss 7, 17, 18, 26, 35, 44, 119.
34. Pss 10–13, 25, 28, 31, 37–39, 41, 55, 58–60, 62, 64, 70, 73, 74, 77, 79, 80, 83, 85, 86, 90, 94, 121, 123, 130, 140–143.

Divination

Throughout ancient Mesopotamia, animal sacrifice was an opportunity to learn about the future. People believed that the gods wrote omens in the entrails of the animal (especially the liver) and even in the animal's behavior beforehand. Any detail, no matter how slight, could be fraught with meaning.

> Typical omens are: if the sheep wiggles its tail; if a sheep paws the ground with its feet; if a sheep's right eye is open and its left eye is closed; if a sheep has tears in its right eye; if a sheep's left ear points toward the slaughter (area); and so forth.[35]

Expert diviners would inspect the entrails of the animal for irregularities in color or shape; archaeologists have found model livers with different regions marked out, indicating how specific markings should be interpreted. The practice was popular across many cultures and lasted thousands of years; the prophet Ezekiel mentions it in connection with the Babylonians.[36] Divination typically provided a "yes/no" answer to some question; offerers asked the gods about every conceivable aspect of life, including military expeditions, health, love, agriculture, and even career plans:

> Šamaš, lord of the judgment, Adad, lord of the inspection, so-and-so, son of so-and-so, who ... has made up his mind, has determined and is aiming to be appointed a temple administrator—your great divinity knows—in accordance with your great divinity should he aim and plan to commission a barber to shave him, to purify him, to cleanse him?[37]

Xenophon, telling about the adventures of a Greek mercenary army in the fourth century BC, describes an occasion when the army was out of supplies and desperate to start their return journey, but the leaders insisted on waiting for a good sacrificial omen.[38] They offered up to three sacrifices a day, each time hoping for a better answer, like a kid who keeps retaking his temperature in the hopes that the thermometer will register a fever high enough to keep him home from school. Eventually they had to resort to buying animals to sacrifice because the army had run out.

---

35. Leichty, "Ritual," 240.
36. Ezek 21:21.
37. Lambert, *Babylonian Oracle Questions*, 53.
38. Xenophon, *Anab.* 6.4.13–22.

What Sacrifice Is Not

What about the Old Testament? That's an easy one: sacrifice has absolutely nothing to do with divination. There's no trace of the idea in any of the ritual procedures described in the Pentateuch, and other laws ban divination in *any* form.[39] The priests did have the mysterious Urim and Thummim,[40] apparently used to ask questions of God,[41] but this was completely separate from sacrifice. King Ahaz, who modified worship at the temple on a pagan model, may have practiced divination in connection with offerings.[42] But for worshippers of the Lord, sacrifice is about the relationship now, not a back door to try to learn what will happen tomorrow.

Penal substitution

I don't know of any Christian theologians who argue that God instituted sacrifice in order to be fed, or to be bribed with gifts, or to give hints about the future. But *many* Christians believe a particular theory of sacrifice that is, in my opinion, mistaken: the penal substitution model.[43] This explanation of sacrifice isn't unique to Christians; it can be found among Jewish interpreters too.[44] But I'll focus here on Christian versions of the idea because it's closely related to how Christians understand the death of Jesus.

Penal substitutionary atonement is a theory of how Jesus' death saves people. It works basically like this: People are sinful. Because God is just, he has to punish them (the "penal" part). Jesus willingly took sinners' place; on the cross, he experienced the punishment that we deserve (the "substitutionary" part). As a result, God and sinners are reconciled (the "atonement" part) because God's justice has been satisfied.

There's a whole cottage industry of books devoted to explaining why penal substitutionary atonement is poor theology. We don't need to recapitulate all that discussion here; the short version is that the New Testament uses many metaphors to describe how Jesus saves us, and penal substitution is a minor one at best. Moreover, the theory gives us a picture of God

---

39. Lev 19:26; Deut 18:10, 14.
40. Exod 28:30.
41. 1 Sam 14:41.
42. 2 Kgs 16:10–16.
43. Gane, *Altar Call*, 110; Gane, *Old Testament Law*, 385–86; Kiuchi, *Leviticus*, 46–47, 61, 82–83, 106; Morales, *Who Shall Ascend?*, 129; Wenham, *Leviticus*, 27–28.
44. Eilberg-Schwartz, *Savage*, 135–36; Ibn Ezra, *Leviticus* 1:4; Levine, *Leviticus*, 21–22, 115–16.

that's inconsistent with scripture as a whole. One of the most well-known verses in the New Testament is "God so loved the world that he gave his only Son,"[45] but, as N. T. Wright observes, penal substitution suggests that "God so *hated* the world, that he *killed* his only son."[46]

When we look at Old Testament sacrifice through penal substitutionary glasses, we come away with some very specific ideas about what it meant. Animal sacrifice involves killing an animal; that death must be a punishment for sins, and the animal takes our place: the animal foreshadows Jesus. Sacrifice creates communion with God by (temporarily, imperfectly) satisfying God's justice; it's a way to deal with human guilt. Sin, in this understanding, becomes What Sacrifice Is All About.

Almost none of this is consistent with the way the Old Testament presents sacrifice. First, not all sacrifices are about sin (more on this in chapter 5). Sin is important, but it's just one clove in the bulb of sacrifice; it's not the whole thing. To be fair, penal substitution doesn't logically require the assumption that all sacrifices are about sin, and some proponents—John Calvin, for example—distinguish between sacrifices for sin and sacrifices for other purposes.[47] But it's not uncommon to find discussions of sacrifice that consider sin and nothing else. *The Life Book*, quoted at the beginning of chapter 2, is a perfect example.

Second, the sacrifices that *do* deal with sin simply don't look like penal substitution. It's not that substitution was unknown in the ancient Near East; on the contrary, some of Israel's neighbors had rituals where the substitutionary aspect was inescapable. The following Hittite ritual is for a king who has seen an omen and thinks trouble is coming for him; his goal is to convince the gods to send the evil after someone or something else instead.

> They drive up to the sanctuary a live steer and consecrate it. The king goes up to the sanctuary and speaks as follows: "That omen which thou gavest, O Moon-god: if thou foundest fault with me and wishedst to behold with thine own eyes the sinner's abasement, see, I, the king, have come in person to thy sanctuary and have given thee these substitutes. Consider the substitution! Let these die! But, let me not die!" They hand the substitutes over . . . and he takes them away. . . .
>
> He brings a healthy prisoner to the sanctuary. They anoint the prisoner with the fine oil of kingship, and he speaks as follows:

---

45. John 3:16.
46. Wright, *Revolution*, 43.
47. Calvin, *Institutes* 4.18.13–16.

> "This man is the king. To him have I given a royal name. Him have I clad in the vestments of kingship. Him have I crowned with the diadem. Remember ye this: That evil omen signifies short years and short days. Pursue ye this substitute!" . . . The one healthy prisoner is released, and he has him taken back to his country.[48]

This goes on for a while, with more substitutes and more prayers at various shrines. (I'm curious to know what the prisoner thought about his role in the proceedings!)

If we're looking for a penal substitutionary ritual, there's no question that this Hittite example is one. But *nothing in the Old Testament remotely resembles this ritual*. Not the sacrificial regulations in Leviticus, not the stories of people offering sacrifices, nothing. Not one psalm expresses gratitude that an animal has died in the psalmist's place. Not one prophet points to sacrificial animals and says, "Remember, this is what you deserve." *It's just not there.*

The Old Testament ritual that most closely resembles the Hittite one—and it's still a stretch—is the Day of Atonement, described in Leviticus 16. This is an annual ceremony for the whole nation that involves fasting, repentance, and a series of special sacrifices. It's the one day in the year when the high priest is allowed to enter the Most Holy Place, the innermost room of the sanctuary where the ark of the covenant sits. Part of the ceremony involves two goats; the high priest casts lots to designate one as a sacrifice and the other as a "scapegoat" (or a goat "for Azazel;" the Hebrew word is not fully understood). After the first goat has been sacrificed, attention turns to the scapegoat:

> Then Aaron shall lay both his hands on the head of the live goat, and confess over it all the iniquities of the people of Israel, and all their transgressions, all their sins, putting them on the head of the goat, and sending it away into the wilderness by means of someone designated for the task. The goat shall bear on itself all their iniquities to a barren region; and the goat shall be set free in the wilderness.[49]

Like the bull and the prisoner in the Hittite ritual, the scapegoat is sent away from the community, and evil is supposed to go with it. But in the Hittite ritual, the king explicitly calls on the Moon-god to send trouble after the substitutes; on the Day of Atonement, it's *the sins themselves* that the

---

48. "Hittite Rituals," trans. Albrecht Goetze, *ANET*, 355.
49. Lev 16:21–22.

scapegoat takes away. I suppose you could infer that, by taking the people's sins outside the camp, the scapegoat is drawing the punishment for those sins after itself too. But the text itself doesn't say this; its focus is on getting rid of sin, not avoiding punishment. Indeed, if punishment is the inevitable consequence of sin, then the two couldn't possibly be separated. Along these lines, we could even conclude that leaving the camp represents a punishment in itself[50]—although, if so, it's worth noting that this punishment stops short of death.

Another similar-looking Hittite ritual has the sacrificers rid themselves of evil using a "scapemouse." They symbolically transfer the evil from themselves to the mouse, and encourage the divine being Alauwaimis to chase after it.

> She wraps up a small piece of tin in the bowstring and attaches it to the sacrificers' right hands and feet. She takes it off them again and attaches it to a mouse with the words: "I have taken the evil off you and transferred it to this mouse. Let this mouse carry it on a long journey to the high mountains, hills and dales!"
>
> She turns the mouse loose saying: "Alauwaimis! This one pursue! I shall give thee a goat to eat!"
>
> She sets up an altar of wood and breaks one long sacrificial loaf for the Alauwaimis gods, she breaks one sacrificial loaf for Alauwaimis, she breaks one sacrificial loaf for Mammas and she puts them upon the altars.
>
> She then consecrates a goat for Alauwaimis saying: "Eat thou!" In front of the loaves she cuts it up and takes off the right shoulder. She cooks it on a fire and puts it in a place apart from the loaves. The liver she offers in the same manner.[51]

Once again, parts of this ritual look superficially similar to things we see in the Old Testament, but other aspects of the ritual are very different. Besides the hint of transactional sacrifice ("I'll give you a goat to eat"), the fact that Alauwaimis is urged to *follow* the scapemouse is the opposite of what we see in Leviticus 16. The purpose of the Day of Atonement isn't to send God into the desert so he'll leave the Israelites alone; it's to deal with the people's sins so that God can stay in the camp *with them.*

Even more important, before we use the scapegoat to explain how other sacrifices work, we need to observe that the scapegoat *isn't even a*

---

50. Sklar, *Leviticus*, 212–13.
51. "Hittite Rituals," trans. Albrecht Goetze, *ANET*, 348.

What Sacrifice Is Not

sacrifice. The *other* goat is the sacrifice! The scapegoat isn't killed at all; it's set free in the wilderness. Some later traditions recall that someone would follow the scapegoat for some distance and push it off a cliff[52]—not because the death of the goat in itself was necessary, but just to make sure the goat didn't wander back into the community. Again, the purpose was to keep the goat away, not to punish it.

So the scapegoat isn't a sacrifice, but on the other hand it's clearly sacrifice-adjacent. Could the hand-leaning ritual be the key that connects them? Recall that the high priest lays two hands on the head of the scapegoat as he confesses the Israelites' sins; this is how he transfers the sins from the people to the goat. And, in fact, hand-leaning happens in most of the other sacrificial rituals described in Leviticus: the offerer lays a hand on the head of the animal before it's killed.[53] So maybe *all* the regular sacrifices involve a transfer of sins to the animal, just like the scapegoat.[54]

The problem with this theory is that it's not clear that hand-leaning for the other sacrifices is the same thing as hand-leaning for the scapegoat. First, the high priest leans two hands on the head of the scapegoat, but for other offerings only one hand is involved. The difference is minor, and some traditions conclude that all sacrifices actually involved two hands,[55] but at least some commentators consider the difference noteworthy.[56] Second, hand-leaning for other sacrifices hasn't universally been understood as a transfer of sins; Philo, for example, interprets the gesture as the offerer publicly declaring that he has a clear conscience.[57]

Third and most notably, hand-leaning is never mentioned for sacrifices of birds or for the *'asham*,[58] an offering brought to atone for certain specific sins. More likely, hand-leaning on ordinary sacrifices expressed, not transference of sin, but ownership:[59] "This sacrifice is for me, not the guy in line behind me." This was unnecessary for birds (or grain offerings), because they would have been carried in the owner's hands anyway. And

---

52. m. Yoma 6:5–6.
53. Lev 1:4; 3:2, 8, 12–13; 4:4, 15, 24, 29.
54. Wenham, *Leviticus*, 61–63.
55. Wright, "Gesture of Hand Placement," 433–34.
56. Ibn Ezra, *Leviticus* 1:4.
57. Philo, *Spec.* 1.202–4.
58. Lev 5.
59. Milgrom, *Leviticus 1–16*, 150–53.

for the *'asham* there was the option of offering money instead of an animal;[60] money, too, would have been carried in the owner's hands. Many Hittite rituals had a hand placement gesture with a similar meaning, especially when a priest or other expert performed the ritual *on behalf of* someone else; hand placement was like "the signature on a letter delivered to the god by means of a [ritual] postman. When the god receives the letter, he recognizes that it is from the one who signed the letter . . . not from the postman who delivered it."[61]

Even if the scapegoat ritual on the Day of Atonement doesn't give us a penal substitutionary theory of sacrifice, could there be clues in the other sacrifices themselves that lead us to the same conclusion? Specifically, what does it mean when a sacrifice leads to "cleansing" or "purification"?[62] The sacrificial system doesn't make much use of the language of punishment, but it makes plenty of use of the language of cleansing; maybe the latter is another way of getting at the same idea. Proponents of penal substitution are often quick to connect the two concepts:

> The sacrifice of expiation is that which is intended to appease God's wrath, to satisfy his judgment, *and so to wash sins and cleanse them* that the sinner, *purged of their filth and restored to the purity of righteousness*, may return into favor with God.[63]

And conversely, some Christians today are wary of purification language, at least in part, because they associate it with penal substitution.[64]

But notice what Calvin does in the passage just quoted. The controlling story is the courtroom drama in which God's justice must be satisfied. What sacrifice (or Jesus) *really* does is satisfy God's wrath, and cleansing is just a way to describe what things look like afterwards. Cleansing is only a metaphor; penal substitution is "what really happened." Incidentally, this is another criticism of penal substitutionary atonement: some proponents believe that it's a complete and fully adequate explanation of the death of Jesus; any other way of telling the story is just an analogy. "Jesus sets us free from slavery to sin; that's because we're like slaves when we have sinned and are subject to God's inevitable wrath." "Jesus reconciles us to God; that's

60. Lev 5:15; 6:6.
61. Wright, "Gesture of Hand Placement," 443.
62. Lev 8:15; 16:19; Ezek 43:18–26; 45:18–20; Luke 5:14; Heb 9:22.
63. Calvin, *Institutes* 4.18.13, emphasis added.
64. Beck, *Unclean*, 36–41.

What Sacrifice Is Not

because God's wrath wouldn't allow us to be in relationship with him until Jesus took the punishment for our sin." J. I. Packer does this explicitly:

> Sometimes the death of Christ is depicted as *reconciliation*, or peace-making after hatred and war (Romans 5:10 f.; 2 Corinthians 5:18 ff.; Colossians 1:20 ff.); sometimes it is depicted as *redemption*, or rescue by ransom from danger and captivity (Romans 3:24; Galatians 3:13, 4:5; 1 Peter 1:18; Revelation 5:9); sometimes it is pictured as a *sacrifice* (Ephesians 5:2; Hebrews 9:1—10:18), an act of *self-giving* (Galatians 1:4, 2:20; 1 Timothy 2:6), *sin-bearing* (John 1:29; 1 Peter 2:24; Hebrews 9:28), and *blood-shedding* (Mark 14:24; Hebrews 9:14; Revelation 1:5). All these thoughts have to do with the putting away of sin and the restoring of unclouded fellowship between man and God, as a glance at the texts mentioned will show; and all of them have as their background the threat of divine judgment which Jesus's death averted. In other words, there are so many pictures and illustrations of the reality of propitiation, viewed from different standpoints. It is a shallow fallacy to imagine, as many scholars unhappily do, that this variety of language must necessarily imply variation of thought.[65]

Even if we want to allow penal substitution to have a place as just one among the many images that the New Testament uses to describe how Jesus saves us, many Christians (myself included) have been so thoroughly trained by our penal substitutionary glasses that it takes conscious effort to see anything else. It's like when you get a shopping cart whose wheels are permanently twisted to the left, and you have to push the thing right just to make it go straight.

Back to the main point. Cleansing language is popular with the penal substitution crowd, but only as a metaphor, not because cleansing is intrinsic to how penal substitution works. And so just because we see cleansing language associated with sacrifices doesn't mean that sacrifice is a penal substitutionary system. In fact, defilement and cleansing is an entirely separate way of thinking about sin.

But if cleansing is its own system with its own logic, how exactly does that logic work? And why is cleansing in the Old Testament so often associated with blood? Digging into the purification system will need its own chapter; let's get to it.

---

65. Packer, *Knowing God*, 171–72.

4

Sin Is like Dirt; Blood Is like Soap

The miasma of sin

The scenery in Salt Lake City is stunning. We have the Wasatch Mountains on the east, so close that parts of the city actually run up into the foothills; world-class skiing is a 30-minute drive away. To the west, a bit further away, we have the Oquirrh Mountains. Aside from narrow gaps at the north and south ends of the valley, there are mountains in literally every direction. When I first moved to Utah, locals would sometimes give directions by saying "drive east, towards the mountains," which was profoundly unhelpful. They meant "towards the *closer* mountains," but to a newcomer they're all close!

But we pay a price for those beautiful views. Because the Salt Lake Valley is basically a giant bowl, sometimes—especially in the winter—a layer of warmer air gets trapped under a layer of cooler air, and all the pollution that we generate gets trapped with it. This is called an inversion, and it means we're stuck with an ugly haze that obscures the sun, irritates our lungs, and can even hide the mountains. We don't just have daily weather forecasts; they come with daily air quality forecasts too. On bad days, schools cancel recess and people in sensitive groups are encouraged to stay inside.

The Old Testament talks about sin in a lot of different ways, and one of the most common ones is to describe sin as impurity. That impurity

Sin Is like Dirt; Blood Is like Soap

turns out to function a lot like air pollution. Sin is a miasma, a contagion that pollutes at a distance, something that hurts the whole community. Sin doesn't just pollute the sinner; it pollutes the whole land. This idea shows up repeatedly in the Old Testament, and receives its fullest expression in Leviticus:

> Do not defile yourselves in any of these ways, for by all these practices the nations I am casting out before you *have defiled themselves*. Thus *the land became defiled*; and I punished it for its iniquity, and the land vomited out its inhabitants. But you shall keep my statutes and my ordinances and commit none of these abominations, either the citizen or the alien who resides among you (for the inhabitants of the land, who were before you, committed all of these abominations, and *the land became defiled*); otherwise the land will vomit you out for defiling it, as it vomited out the nation that was before you.[1]

This is a communal view of sin that's all too often neglected in individualistic western cultures. Many Christians tend to think about sin as a personal matter between me and God, but scripture understands that sin is bigger than that: it's *both* personal *and* corporate. A parent's addiction isn't just a private problem when it harms other members of the family. A man who downloads child sexual abuse images (a more accurate term than "child porn") alone in his home is supporting an industry that exploits and traumatizes children. The evil of racism isn't lessened just because some particular harm is embedded in "the system" as opposed to being the result of clear, discrete actions by identifiable individuals. Our failure to be good stewards of God's creation affects people we will never meet, whether they live downstream along a river we're polluting or in a low-lying coastal area threatened by climate change.

The Leviticus passage could not be more clear that God's big, beautiful, interconnected world is affected by human sin, and that God takes this very seriously. The passage also does something else that's pretty remarkable: it describes the land itself as an agent; the land will vomit out the people who pollute it. And the idea that the land can actively do stuff isn't unique to this passage. Later in Leviticus, when God describes the dire consequences that await Israel if they fail to follow him—up to and including exile, being vomited out—he emphasizes that "the land shall rest, and enjoy its sabbath years. As long as it lies desolate, it shall have the rest it did not have on

---

1. Lev 18:24–28, emphasis added.

your sabbaths when you were living on it."[2] When the people of Judah were finally carried off into exile in Babylon, the prophet Ezekiel preached to his fellow exiles in the name of God that this was precisely what had happened: they polluted the land, and now they were suffering the consequences.

> So I poured out my wrath upon them for the blood that they had shed upon the land, and for the idols with which they had defiled it. I scattered them among the nations, and they were dispersed through the countries; in accordance with their conduct and their deeds I judged them.[3]

To the Israelites' neighbors, this idea wasn't necessarily strange. Talking about sin as a kind of pollution wasn't a foreign concept in the ancient Near East.[4] Wrong actions—especially serious crimes, like murder—could pollute a person and even the whole city.[5] But the idea is definitely strange in many western contexts today; most of the time, we just don't think this way. And even when we do talk about sin as a kind of impurity, it's all too common to do so for sexual sins *and no others*—in stark contrast to scripture, where idolatry, murder, and greed are sources of pollution too.[6] All of this means that many of us aren't naturally equipped to enter the thought-world of Old Testament law; we'll need to rely heavily on our imaginations. But the payoff is that we'll understand more clearly what scripture is trying to tell us: the defiling force of sin is bigger than just one person or just one kind of misdeed; it's as big as all the brokenness that spoils God's good creation.

The *chatta't* and *The Picture of Dorian Gray*

The land isn't the only thing that sin pollutes. God's sanctuary, his dwelling place that "remains with [the people] in the midst of their uncleannesses,"[7] is especially vulnerable. Horrific practices such as child sacrifice are explicitly said to pollute the sanctuary:

---

2. Lev 26:34b–35.
3. Ezek 36:18–19.
4. Attridge, "Pollution," 71–83.
5. Parker, *Miasma*, ch. 4.
6. Ezek 37:23; Num 35:33; Mark 7:22.
7. Lev 16:16.

Sin Is like Dirt; Blood Is like Soap

> I myself will set my face against them, and will cut them off from the people, because they have given of their offspring to Molech, *defiling my sanctuary* and profaning my holy name.[8]

Logically enough, if the sanctuary can be polluted, there are rituals to purify it. On the Day of Atonement, the priest takes the blood of the sacrificed goat and puts it on the altar; this action cleanses the altar.[9] Similarly, Moses purifies the altar with the blood of a sacrifice during the inauguration ceremony for the high priest Aaron and his sons.[10]

The sacrifice that accomplishes this is the *chatta't* (that first sound is the *ch* of *Chanukkah*, not of *change*). The *chatta't* is often translated as the "sin offering," but we'll soon see that "purification offering" is a better translation. First, though, let's take a closer look at exactly what the *chatta't* purifies.

Leviticus 4 describes four variations on the *chatta't*, depending on who sinned. If the sinner is an individual, the blood from the *chatta't* is placed on the altar of burnt offering,[11] the big altar in front of the sanctuary where sacrifices are burned. (A ruler has to bring a male goat, while a commoner brings a female goat or sheep. This may be something like a sliding scale; it's possible that people who weren't wealthy were more likely to have females to spare than males.[12] Philo believes that the commoner brings a female because the commoner and the female are both inferior.[13] I have no comment on this.)

But for sins of the high priest, or sins of the whole people, the blood of the *chatta't* goes further. The high priest takes some of the blood into the sanctuary itself; he sprinkles it in front of the curtain that separates the Holy Place from the Most Holy Place, and puts it on the horns of the incense altar in the Holy Place.[14] The pollution from these more serious community sins is stronger; it reaches deeper into the sanctuary, so the purifying blood has to follow it there.

Finally, on the Day of Atonement, the high priest brings blood from the *chatta't* into the Most Holy Place itself. The Day of Atonement is like

---

8. Lev 20:3, emphasis added.
9. Lev 16:18–19.
10. Lev 8:14–15.
11. Lev 4:22–25, 27–30.
12. Kamionkowski, *Leviticus*, 35–36; Milgrom, *Leviticus 1–16*, 252.
13. Philo, *Spec.* 1.228–29.
14. Lev 4:3–7, 13–18.

spring cleaning, when the sanctuary is purified inside and out from even the most serious sins.

This pattern illustrates how sin contaminates at a distance. There's just no way an idolatrous or violent Israelite (at least, anyone other than a priest) could have polluted the incense altar in the Holy Place by contact, let alone anything in the Most Holy Place. Sin isn't like mud that the sinner literally wipes onto an altar or some other holy object; it's like dirty air that disperses without direct contact. And the sanctuary, like Salt Lake residents with asthma or COPD, is especially sensitive to this pollution.

Jacob Milgrom, who offered the first and best modern articulation of this metaphor that is latent in the text, compares this view of sin and the sanctuary to Oscar Wilde's novel *The Picture of Dorian Gray*.[15] In Wilde's story, a young man's portrait has magical powers: it ages, but he doesn't. Dorian Gray decides this is great—he can do whatever he wants, with no consequences. He hides the portrait and lives licentiously, fooling everyone he meets with his young and innocent appearance. By the end of the story, the portrait shows a broken, diseased man with cruelty written plainly on his face. (Spoiler alert: there are consequences after all.)

In the theology of Leviticus, we might not be able to see how sin pollutes the sinner—but sin will *definitely* leave its mark on the sanctuary. In Milgrom's memorable words, sin is "an aerial miasma that possesse[s] magnetic attraction for the realm of the sacred."[16] The sanctuary is a barometer for the whole community; even if we don't see our accumulated sin, God does. God is willing to tolerate these impurities for a time, but if they build up too much, they will drive him out. And so the eventual consequence of sin is that God's presence will leave.

This is precisely the drama of the book of Ezekiel. Early in the book, God makes it clear that sin has accumulated to a crisis point. In one vision, God shows Ezekiel the idols that the leaders have put in the temple and asks, "[D]o you see what they are doing, the great abominations that the house of Israel are committing here, *to drive me far from my sanctuary*?"[17] Then, in chapter 10, Ezekiel watches as "the glory of the LORD"—a wild vision of a fiery figure, supernatural creatures, and "wheels within wheels"—comes out of the temple, crosses the threshold, and stops at the east gate of the

---

15. Milgrom, "Israel's Sanctuary," 397–98.
16. Milgrom, *Leviticus 1–16*, 257.
17. Ezek 8:6, emphasis added.

Sin Is like Dirt; Blood Is like Soap

temple complex.[18] We're teetering on the edge of a precipice: Will God actually leave his people? Have things really gone that far?

Then God shows Ezekiel some of the most violent leaders of the people, who "have killed many in this city, and have filled its streets with the slain."[19] God speaks a word of judgment against the city; it will be conquered by enemies and the people driven into exile. But then, addressing those who are *already* living in exile, he speaks an unexpected word of hope:

> Though I removed them far away among the nations, yet I have been a sanctuary to them for a little while in the countries where they have gone. Therefore say: Thus says the Lord God: I will gather you from the peoples, and assemble you out of the countries where you have been scattered, and I will give you the land of Israel. When they come there, they will remove from it all its detestable things and all its abominations. I will give them one heart, and put a new spirit within them; I will remove the heart of stone from their flesh and give them a heart of flesh, so that they may follow my statutes and keep my ordinances and obey them. Then they shall be my people, and I will be their God.[20]

Hope isn't lost. God hasn't given up on his people completely, and he promises a day when he'll bring the exiles back; they will clean out the temple, once again making it fit for God's presence, so they can live in community once more.

But all this is a vision of the future. For now, it's too late: God's presence rises up and leaves the city.[21] Everything that was threatened has finally come to pass; the sanctuary is polluted, and God has abandoned it.

There is power in the blood

We've seen that the *chatta't*'s job is to purify a sanctuary polluted by sin. But how it does this is still something of a mystery. The ritual procedures of Leviticus 4 (ordinary *chatta't*s) and 16 (the Day of Atonement) rely heavily on blood: putting it on the altar or sprinkling it in a holy place. It certainly sounds like blood is the thing that cleanses the sanctuary. Why blood?

---

18. Ezek 10:18–19.
19. Ezek 11:6.
20. Ezek 11:16–20.
21. Ezek 11:22–23.

Penal substitutionary atonement has a ready answer. The animal is killed in place of the sinner, taking the punishment the sinner deserves; the blood represents that vicarious death.[22] Putting the blood in important places around the sanctuary is a visual representation of the fact that punishment has been inflicted, God's justice has been satisfied, and God's wrath has been appeased.[23] Does the blood ritual mean that sacrifices operate on the penal substitutionary model after all?

Actually, no. Remember, according to strict penal substitution, the blood is still just a metaphor, a physical reminder of what *really* matters: the death of the animal. The whole idea of "cleansing" itself is just a figure of speech. But Leviticus does *not* treat the cleansing power of sacrifice as a metaphor.[24] It may not be physical—it's not clear to me that the priests thought there were tiny sin particles stuck to the altar—but the principles of justice in penal substitutionary atonement aren't physical either! Pollution and cleansing aren't decorative figures of speech that Leviticus uses around the periphery of the real system; they *are* the system.

One place we can see the importance of cleansing from sin is in the way the Old Testament describes it. There are a few Hebrew verbs used to mean "cleanse" or "purify," and one of them—*chitte'*—comes from the root that means "sin." When Moses purifies the altar during Aaron's inauguration, this is the word that's used: " . . . and Moses took the blood, and he put it on the horns of the altar all around with his finger, and he 'sinned' the altar."[25] Moses isn't sinning against the altar; rather, we're seeing a verb form that means "remove the thing." English has this construction too: When we "weed" a garden, we're removing the weeds from the garden. When we "peel" an apple, we're removing the peel from the apple. When we "dust" a shelf, we're removing the dust from the shelf. When Moses "sins" the altar, *he's removing the sin from the altar*. He's "de-sinning" it.

This is why the NIV, NRSV, KJV, and other translations use "purify" or "cleanse" to translate this verb (as well as other Hebrew verbs with related meanings). It's also why "purification offering" is a better translation than "sin offering" for *chatta't*, which involves the same root. It's the "de-sinning" offering; the emphasis is on its function as a way to cleanse impurities, some of which are caused by sin (and some of which are unrelated to sin; more

---

22. Packer, *Knowing God*, 168–69.
23. Wenham, *Leviticus*, 80.
24. Klawans, *Impurity and Sin*, 32–36.
25. Lev 8:15a, my translation.

Sin Is like Dirt; Blood Is like Soap

on this in chapter 6). At any rate, the governing theory of these sacrifices is clear: *sin is like dirt; blood is like soap*. Supernatural dirt, to be sure; it contaminates from a distance like air pollution, while cleansing happens up close with sprinkling and wiping. But we don't have to equate sin with exactly one kind of physical dirt in order to see the point.

All this still doesn't explain why *blood*, of all things, is the soap. In a little bit we'll discuss one way of understanding what makes blood special. But I think to a large degree we just have to accept that blood-as-detergent was simply part of the general background knowledge of the ancient Near East. It wasn't just Israel; many cultures had ritual practices that relied on blood to cleanse people or places. For example, as part of the Babylonian Akitu festival, a *mašmaššu* (priest) has to purify rooms in the temple to get them ready for visiting gods. He does this by wiping them down with several things, including the carcass of a decapitated ram. When he's all done, he throws the ram's body in the river like a used sponge.

> [T]he *mašmaššu* enters the Ezida, the cella of Nabu. He purifies the temple with censer and torch and *egubbû*-vessel. He sprinkles water from the Tigris and Euphrates cisterns. He anoints the doors of the entire chamber with cedar oil. In the middle of the court of the cella, he places a silver censer. On top he mixes perfumes and cypress. He summons the slaughterer. He decapitates a ram. The *mašmaššu* wipes the temple with the carcass of the ram. He recites the incantations for exorcising the temple. He purifies the whole cella including its surrounding areas and then takes down the censer. The *mašmaššu* takes up the carcass of that ram and goes to the river. He sets his face westward and throws the carcass of that ram into the river.[26]

The cleansing function of blood is perfectly clear here, and some Hittite ritual texts lay it out even more explicitly: "They smear with blood the golden god, the wall, and the utensils of the entirely new god. The new god and the temple become clean."[27]

The Greeks made use of this idea too. Slaughtered animals might be carried around a place of assembly to purify it and get it ready for a meeting, or around a whole city to purify it after it was contaminated by murderers.[28] The Macedonian army used to sacrifice a dog to create "an 'absorptive zone'

---

26. Wright, *Disposal of Impurity*, 63–64.
27. Wright, *Disposal of Impurity*, 36, footnote 67.
28. Parker, *Miasma*, 21–22.

Misreading Ritual

for all its impurities."[29] The epic story of Jason and the Argonauts includes a scene where Jason, polluted because he has committed murder, is purified with pig's blood and a sacrifice.[30]

If you think this is all just plain weird, you're not alone. An observation attributed to the fourth-century BC philosopher Heraclitus complains that people "vainly try to purify themselves with blood when defiled with it, as if one who had stepped into mud were to wash it off with mud."[31] But for many people in the ancient Near East, this was perfectly normal. Cleansing wasn't necessarily the *only* function of blood (or even its primary function[32]), but it was a *possible* function of blood.[33] By adopting blood purification as part of the sacrificial system, God was speaking the Israelites' language.

But this doesn't mean scripture has no theology of blood whatsoever. We'll need a couple more chapters to lay the foundation for a fuller discussion; for now, let's preview a crucial passage from Leviticus 17. This is the closest the Old Testament comes to explaining why blood acts like soap—and it's not in the context of sacrificial regulations, but rather after a law against eating blood:

> If anyone of the house of Israel or of the aliens who reside among them eats any blood, I will set my face against that person who eats blood, and will cut that person off from the people. For the life of the flesh is in the blood; and I have given it to you for making atonement for your lives on the altar; for, as life, it is the blood that makes atonement.[34]

The primary point here is that God does not permit people to eat meat with the blood in it, a prohibition that goes back to Noah[35] and that was consistently interpreted as applying to all people, not just Jews. (It was one of the few "ritual" requirements of Old Testament law that the early church applied to Gentile converts as well.[36]) The idea is that the life of the animal belongs to God; although God allows people to eat meat as a

---

29. Parker, *Miasma*, 22.
30. Apollonius, *Argon.* 4.662–717.
31. Heraclitus, DK 5.
32. McCarthy, "Symbolism," 166–76.
33. Stowers, "Comparison," 184–87; Wright, *Disposal of Impurity*, 34–36.
34. Lev 17:10–11.
35. Gen 9:3–5.
36. Acts 15:22–29.

concession, eating the blood disrespects this fact, an appropriation of life that is not ours to take. Earlier in Leviticus 17, as well as in the Genesis passage, God says that anyone who doesn't treat blood properly is guilty of "bloodshed"[37]—murder.

We'll discuss the link between blood and purification further in chapter 7, and the connection to diet in chapter 8. For now, notice that the foundation of the sacrificial system is *life*—not punishment, not wrath, but life. This is the core of the relationship between a holy people and the "God of the living."[38]

I've emphasized the corporate aspects of the *chatta't*, but of course the Old Testament understands the individual nature of sin too. Recognizing communal sin doesn't mean we can ignore individual sin, or vice versa. It's helpful for those of us who were brought up in an individualistic culture to pay special attention to the way Leviticus imagines sin polluting the community as a whole—as an addition to conceptions of individual sin, not a replacement. Commentators recognize both dynamics in the *chatta't*. Nachmanides speaks of the *chatta't* purifying "a stain upon the soul;"[39] whether and how the *chatta't* purifies the altar, the sinner, or both remains an area of vigorous scholarly debate.[40]

Finally, I've argued that, in the world of the Old Testament, the cleansing effected by sacrifice is very real. But this isn't the same as saying that sacrifice works mechanically, or that it works automatically. The *chatta't* isn't a guaranteed route to forgiveness; the tirades of Isaiah, Amos, and others noted in chapter 2 show that the prophets understood this very well. That sacrifice (or any other religious activity) can't substitute for repentance, ethical action, and the worshipper's inner disposition has always been clear Jewish teaching.[41] Rabbi J. H. Hertz even suggests that most of the *chatta't* was discarded, rather than burned and given to God as smoke, to avoid suggesting that the sinner could purchase God's forgiveness.[42] Philo puts it well:

---

37. Lev 17:3–4.
38. Matt 22:32.
39. Nachmanides, *Leviticus* 4:2.
40. Gane, *Cult and Character*; Gane, "Privative Preposition מן," 209–22; Vis, "Purgation of Persons," 33–57; Willis, *Leviticus*, 39–40.
41. Riskin, *Vayikra*, 30.
42. Hertz, *Pentateuch and Haftorahs*, 418.

> [F]or if the man who made the offerings was foolish and ignorant, the sacrifices were no sacrifices, the victims were not sacred or hallowed, the prayers were ill-omened, and liable to be answered by utter destruction, for even when they appear to be received, they produce no remission of sins but only a reminding of them.
>
> But if the man who offers the sacrifice be bold and just, then the sacrifice remains firm, even if the flesh of the victim be consumed, or rather, I might say, even if no victim be offered up at all....[43]

Pollution and the wrath of God

Some Christians, at certain times and certain places, grow up hearing a lot about the wrath of God. I didn't. I've spent most of my time in circles where God's wrath is heavily de-emphasized in favor of God's love, where we're sensitive to those among us who have been hurt by leaders wielding God's wrath as a weapon, where its existence in scripture is somewhat inconvenient or maybe even embarrassing.

I believe that emphasizing God's love over God's wrath is right, and that it's fundamentally scriptural. This is, after all, the theme of the great confession repeated throughout the Old Testament: that God is "merciful and gracious, slow to anger, and abounding in steadfast love and faithfulness."[44] But judgment is unavoidably part of the story too, and sometimes—perhaps surprisingly to us—people actually seem *excited* about it. Consider Psalm 98, which ends with a crescendo of praise that includes all creation:

> Make a joyful noise to the Lord, all the earth;
>   break forth into joyous song and sing praises.
> Sing praises to the Lord with the lyre,
>   with the lyre and the sound of melody.
> With trumpets and the sound of the horn
>   make a joyful noise before the King, the Lord.
> Let the sea roar, and all that fills it;
>   the world and those who live in it.
> Let the floods clap their hands;
>   let the hills sing together for joy
> at the presence of the Lord, for he is coming
>   to judge the earth.

43. Philo, *Mos.* 2.107–8 (Yonge).
44. Exod 34:6.

> He will judge the world with righteousness,
>> and the peoples with equity.[45]

And why is everyone rejoicing? Because they expect God to come and judge the world!

In the Salt Lake Valley, when we have a bad inversion, it can take days or even weeks to clear out. But there's one thing that will scrub the air quickly: a storm. When we're desperate for a clear view of the sun, or a literal breath of fresh air, we start wishing for a good storm to blow through and clean up.

This is what the authors of scripture are doing when they long for God's wrath to blow through and set things right. They look around and see the stain of sin everywhere: oppression, injustice, discord, brokenness. The problems seem so great, and human strength seems so inadequate to face them. Another psalmist imagines God judging all the other so-called gods we're tempted to worship; his verdict is damning:

> God has taken his place in the divine council;
>> in the midst of the gods he holds judgment:
>
> "How long will you judge unjustly
>> and show partiality to the wicked?
>
> Give justice to the weak and the orphan;
>> maintain the right of the lowly and the destitute. . . ."
>
> Rise up, O God, judge the earth;
>> for all the nations belong to you![46]

When the psalmists long for God's judgment, that's because they trust God's goodness. A God who isn't angry at sex trafficking or racism or domestic abuse, a God who's just fine with selfishness and greed and arrogance and indifference, is not a God worthy of worship.

The problem with a storm in the Salt Lake Valley, though, is that it isn't a permanent solution. A storm can come through and clear up an inversion, but the inversion may just come right back, because we keep putting more pollution in the air. The final judgment of God, the kind envisioned in Revelation, isn't a little weather system that moves through the valley in a few hours. To *really* deal with evil, God's wrath has to remove the *causes* of evil. It has to be a hurricane that overturns our cars and knocks down our factories and floods our power plants so that the air *stays* clean.

---

45. Ps 98:4–9.
46. Ps 82:1–3, 8.

And this is why God's wrath is also scary. I want to breathe clean air, but I don't want to give up my car or the electricity in my home. Any part of me that's selfish or greedy, that benefits from harming others, must be burned up in the fire of God's judgment. If I've devoted my life to building a predatory payday loan company, that accomplishment will have no place in God's kingdom. If I get my self-worth from lording it over others, then a heaven of mutual submission and love will seem like hell.

The good news is that, even though the process of dealing with sin can be painful, we can trust God that the ultimate outcome will be good. Furthermore, we can trust that God won't abandon his people forever. The prophet Ezekiel saw a vision of God leaving the temple because it was so polluted, and soon the temple was literally destroyed by the Babylonians. But the book ends with a vision of a new temple, clean and fresh and thoroughly de-sinned, and a glorious return of the presence of God:

> Then he brought me to the gate, the gate facing east. And there, the glory of the God of Israel was coming from the east; the sound was like the sound of mighty waters; and the earth shone with his glory. The vision I saw was like the vision that I had seen when he came to destroy the city, and like the vision that I had seen by the river Chebar; and I fell upon my face. As the glory of the LORD entered the temple by the gate facing east, the spirit lifted me up, and brought me into the inner court; and the glory of the LORD filled the temple. . . .
>
> He said to me: Mortal, this is the place of my throne and the place for the soles of my feet, where I will reside among the people of Israel forever.[47]

---

47. Ezek 43:1–5, 7.

5

NOT ALL SACRIFICES ARE ABOUT SIN

WE'VE JUST SPENT a whole chapter exploring how one type of sacrifice, the *chatta't*, takes away sin—not by killing an innocent animal in place of a guilty sinner, but by using blood like soap to clean up the pollution of sin. This model of the *chatta't* leads us to understand sin more fully: as a problem that's both individual and corporate, and as a problem that needs not just forgiveness but also cleansing and healing. It also helps us make sense of the way scripture talks about sin, the sanctuary, and the presence of God.

But recall the analogy from chapter 3: sacrifice is like giving flowers; it's a part of a cultural repertoire that can mean many different things, depending on the context. This analogy makes no sense if it turns out that all sacrifices are about sin. Chapter 3 described several things that Old Testament sacrifice is not; so, besides a way to deal with sin, what else *is* it?

This chapter explores other types of sacrifice described in the Old Testament, beyond the *chatta't*. Some, like the *'asham*, do deal with sin, albeit with a different emphasis. Others, like the *'olah* and the *shelamim*, have to do with entirely different aspects of the relationship between God and his people. When we put all these types of sacrifice together, we get a rich and beautiful picture of a God who chooses to relate to his people in many ways, and a people who are so eager to draw near to God that they do so in all kinds of circumstances: in joy and in grief, at set times and spontaneously, individually and in community.

As we look at various types of sacrifice, we should keep in mind that the rituals described in Leviticus do *not* necessarily match what people actually did. The Old Testament itself tells stories of unauthorized sacrificial procedure,[1] and certainly plenty would have happened in Israel's centuries-long existence that simply isn't recorded. And even if the rules of Leviticus were followed to the letter, it's unlikely that all worshippers—or even priests!—had the same beliefs about what was going on. (Compare the wide variety of ways Christian churches observe the Lord's supper. And even within a single church, individual Christians have many different theological interpretations of what it means.)

In fact, this diversity of interpretation extends even to the fundamental point of this chapter. I will argue that not all sacrifices are about sin, but it's only fair to point out that there are commentators, both Jewish and Christian, who disagree. For example, Nachmanides, a Jewish commentator living a generation after Maimonides, describes the purpose of the *'olah* in terms that look remarkably like penal substitutionary atonement:

> [A] person should realize that he has sinned against his G-d with his body and his soul, and that "his" blood should really be spilled and "his" body burned, were it not for the loving-kindness of the Creator, Who took from him a substitute and a ransom, namely this offering, so that its blood should be in place of his blood, its life in place of his life, and that the chief limbs of the offering should be in place of the chief parts of his body.[2]

Rabbi J. H. Hertz doesn't use a penal substitutionary model, but agrees that even the *'olah* and *shelamim* deal with sin.[3] And, of course, in chapter 3 we saw examples of Christian commentators who interpret all sacrifices as penal substitution.

But this perspective is by no means universal. Many other commentators interpret at least some sacrifices as being about something other than sin—or, at least, as representing something *in addition to* sin. Either way, there's a long tradition of understanding that resolving sin isn't the only thing sacrifices do.

These other dimensions of sacrifice have been interpreted in many ways. Rabbi Jonathan Sacks observes that allowing them to offer gifts is one way God gives dignity to his children.[4] Hugo Grotius summarizes the

---

1. Lev 10:1–2; 1 Sam 2:12–17; 1 Kgs 22:43; 2 Chr 26:16–20; Isa 65:2–5.
2. Nachmanides, *Leviticus* 1:9.
3. Hertz, *Pentateuch and Haftorahs*, 411–12, 415.
4. Sacks, *Leviticus*, 61–69.

purpose of sacrifice as "praises, prayers, and blessings."[5] Joseph Albo, a fifteenth-century Jewish philosopher, suggests that when the worshipper sees the animal burned up on the altar, he remembers his own mortality—and therefore he rededicates himself to doing good.[6] Maimonides argues that the purpose of sacrifice was to wean the Israelites off of idolatry.[7] Philo interprets the hand-leaning gesture as declaring a clear conscience; he describes an attitude (at least for the 'olah) that would be unthinkable for someone coming to have his sins forgiven:

> Again, the hands which are laid upon the head of the victim are a most manifest symbol of irreproachable actions, and of a life which does nothing which is open to accusation, but which in all respects is passed in a manner consistent with the laws and ordinances of nature; for the law, in the first place, desires that the mind of the man who is offering the sacrifice shall be made holy by being exercised in good and advantageous doctrines; and, in the second place, that his life shall consist of most virtuous actions, so that, in conjunction with the imposition of hands, the man may speak freely out of his cleanly conscience, and may say, "These hands have never received any gift as a bribe to commit an unjust action, nor any division of what has been obtained by rapine or by covetousness, nor have they shed innocent blood, nor have they wrought mutilation, nor works of insolence, nor acts of violence, nor have they inflicted any wounds; nor, in fact, have they performed any action whatever which is liable to accusation or to reproach, but have been ministers in everything which is honourable and advantageous, and which is honoured by wisdom, or by the laws, or by honourable and virtuous men."[8]

Similarly, Philo argues that the reason the animal has to be physically perfect is to teach worshippers to approach God with perfect souls.[9]

Christian commentators, too, offer a dizzying variety of interpretations of sacrifice—only some of which are related to sin. David Chytraeus, a sixteenth-century theologian, foregrounds penal substitution but also finds room for an understanding that sacrifices express thanksgiving, teach

---

5. Grotius, *Annotata*, 88.
6. Albo, *Book of Principles* 3.25.14.
7. Maimonides, *Guide* 3.32.
8. Philo, *Spec.* 1.202–4 (Yonge).
9. Philo, *Spec.* 1.167.

obedience, and model holy living:[10] "the variety of Christ's benefits and of spiritual sacrifices were foreshadowed by this diversity of sacrificial types."[11] Allegorical interpretations were especially popular from the early church fathers through medieval times; as we'll see, no detail of the sacrificial ritual was too small to symbolize some profound spiritual truth.

The first seven chapters of Leviticus describe four major types of sacrifice: the *'olah*, the *shelamim*, the *chatta't*, and the *'asham*. We've already discussed the *chatta't* in some detail; the next several sections explore the other three. Then we'll branch out to other types of sacrifice (subtypes of the "big four" and sacrifices for special occasions), and conclude with discussions of atonement and of Jesus as the lamb of God.

The *'asham*: Setting things right

The *chatta't* and the *'asham* are the last two sacrifices introduced in Leviticus 1–7: the *chatta't* occupies Leviticus 4:1—5:13, and the *'asham* Leviticus 5:14—6:7. (The rest of chapter 6, and all of chapter 7, review the sacrifices again with special instructions for the priests.) But since we've already begun out of order with the *chatta't*, we'll continue with the closely related *'asham*.

Like the *chatta't*, the *'asham* is brought for some wrongdoing. Leviticus specifies three scenarios: misusing or defiling a holy thing,[12] robbing or defrauding someone and lying about it under oath,[13] or violating a prohibitive commandment.[14] What's striking about the *'asham* is that, at least in the first and second cases, the sacrifice doesn't stand alone: the offerer also has to make restitution to the priest or the person who was defrauded, paying the full amount of the property plus a 20 percent penalty:

> When any of you commit a trespass and sin unintentionally in any of the holy things of the LORD, you shall bring, as your guilt offering [*'asham*] to the LORD, a ram without blemish from the flock, convertible into silver by the sanctuary shekel; it is a guilt offering [*'asham*]. And you shall make restitution for the holy thing

---

10. Chytraeus, *On Sacrifice*, 43–62.
11. Chytraeus, *On Sacrifice*, 52.
12. Lev 5:15.
13. Lev 6:2–3.
14. Lev 5:17.

in which you were remiss, and shall add one-fifth to it and give it to the priest.[15]

In other words, the *'asham* deals with sin, but it's about more than just personal forgiveness for the sinner; it's about *setting things right*. This is why some scholars prefer the translation "reparation offering,"[16] although the traditional translation is "guilt offering" because the Hebrew word *'asham* comes from a root meaning "guilt."

In this context, it becomes clear that Jesus' teaching about reconciliation wasn't a radical departure from an impersonal Old Testament law; it was a fresh emphasis on principles that were there all along. Jesus taught that we should make things right with a brother or sister before bringing a sacrifice, even to the point of leaving the sacrifice at the altar to go reconcile with a brother or sister first.[17] This looks a lot like the law of the *'asham*, which strongly implies that the person who defrauds a neighbor has to make restitution *before* bringing the sacrifice:

> [W]hen you have sinned and realize your guilt, and would restore what you took by robbery or by fraud or the deposit that was committed to you, or the lost thing that you found, or anything else about which you have sworn falsely, you shall repay the principal amount and shall add one-fifth to it. You shall pay it to its owner when you realize your guilt. And you shall bring to the priest, as your guilt offering [*'asham*] to the LORD, a ram without blemish from the flock, or its equivalent, for a guilt offering [*'asham*].[18]

There's reason to think that the *'asham* may have had an additional function besides righting concrete wrongs. Most translations have a commandment to bring an *'asham* when "you have incurred guilt"[19] or when you "realize your guilt."[20] But that verb—from the same root as *'asham* —can also mean "feel guilty."[21] And "feel guilty" makes excellent sense in context; the sins of fraud and deceit described in Leviticus 6:2–3 are deliberate, so it's hard to understand how the person who does such a thing would later "realize his guilt." The fact that those actions were wrong would have been

15. Lev 5:15–16a.
16. Milgrom, *Leviticus 1–16*, 339–45.
17. Matt 5:23–24.
18. Lev 6:4–6.
19. Lev 5:17.
20. Lev 6:4.
21. Milgrom, *Leviticus 1–16*, 342–45.

obvious from the start! It's probably not that the person later figures out that he did something wrong; more likely, he starts paying attention to his conscience and feels remorse. Moreover, there's no hint in this passage that the wrongdoer got caught; the *'asham* isn't a penalty imposed by a court once the fraud is uncovered. Rather, the initiative comes from the remorseful sinner himself.

All this suggests a dual function for the *'asham*: not only does it provide a framework for making restitution, but it also offers a concrete course of action for worshippers wrestling with a guilty conscience. Philo understands the *'asham* in precisely this way:

> [If w]hen he appears to have escaped all conviction at the hands of his accusers, shall himself become his own accuser, being convicted by his own conscience residing within, and shall reproach himself for the things which he has denied, and as to which he has sworn falsely, and shall come and openly confess the sin which he has committed, and implore pardon; then pardon shall be given to such a man, who shows the truth of his repentance, not by promises but by works. . . .[22]

Philo wasn't alone. In fact, this function goes beyond cases where a person feels guilty about a definite sin after the fact, and extends to people who feel uneasy but aren't sure whether they've actually sinned in the first place. The rabbis recognized an entire category of *'asham*, the *'asham taluy* ("suspended *'asham*"), for situations where a person isn't certain whether he has sinned or not.[23] Anxiety about accidental sins was common in the ancient Near East; Hittite rulers, for example, used elaborate divination procedures when they were afraid that a god was angry at them but didn't know why:

> "The . . . feast has been neglected; the . . . sun-disc has not been decorated." The oracle declared that the god was angry about this, but it was not the only thing. "Since this has again turned out unfavourably, is the god angry because they have sacrificed too late to the god? If so, let the omens be unfavourable." (Result:) unfavourable. . . . So we questioned the temple-servants again, and they said: "A dog came into the temple and upset the table and threw down the sacrificial bread. Is the god angry about that?" (Result:) unfavourable.[24]

22. Philo, *Spec.* 1.235–36 (Yonge).
23. m. Ker. 6:3.
24. Gurney, *Hittites*, 159–60.

This kind of anxiety brings to mind the Athenians' altar "to an unknown god."[25] In a world where the gods might get mad at you for the slightest infraction, where any misfortune might be a sign of divine wrath, this sacrifice starts to look like a gift, not a punishment. It's not just that God is saying "You ought to feel guilty about such-and-such, and you should take these steps to repair the situation." (God does plenty of that in scripture, and with good reason!) But here it's as though God is also saying, "I know you *already* feel guilty; telling you to just stop feeling that way isn't helpful, so let me give you something concrete to do."

When Christians think of Jesus' death as a sacrifice, the *chatta't*—influenced by the discussion of Hebrews 9:1—10:22—may seem like the most obvious point of comparison. After all, the cleansing blood of the *chatta't* looks exactly like the blood of Jesus that sprinkles our hearts clean[26] and washes the robes of the saints.[27] But the *'asham* has something to teach us about Jesus too. In fact, one of the Servant Songs of Isaiah, which Christians have traditionally interpreted as prefigurations of Christ, explicitly calls the servant an *'asham*:

> When you make his life an offering for sin [*'asham*],
>   he shall see his offspring, and shall prolong his days;
> through him the will of the LORD shall prosper.
>   Out of his anguish he shall see light;
> he shall find satisfaction through his knowledge.
>   The righteous one, my servant, shall make many righteous,
> and he shall bear their iniquities.[28]

The consistent message of the New Testament is that Jesus truly is the one who can "make many righteous"—the one who renews, restores, and reconciles; the one who inaugurates the new creation; the one through whom we can become "the righteousness of God."[29] Like the *'asham*, Jesus is the concrete assurance that God is for us.[30]

---

25. Acts 17:23.
26. Heb 10:19–22.
27. Rev 7:14.
28. Isa 53:10b–11.
29. 2 Cor 5:17–21.
30. Rom 8:31.

The *'olah*: Complete self-giving

Now we come to the place where Leviticus starts: the *'olah* (plural *'olot*). The *'olah* is the only sacrifice that's always completely burned (except for the skin); for this reason, it's usually translated as the "burnt offering." The Hebrew term *'olah* comes from a verb that means "go up," most likely in reference to the way the entire offering figuratively goes up to God in smoke; an alternative translation is "ascension offering."[31]

It makes perfect sense for Leviticus to describe the *'olah* first because, in a lot of ways, it seems to be the basic or default offering. In some of the earliest stories of sacrifice, Noah[32] and Abraham[33] are described as offering an *'olah*; Moses uses the term to tell Pharaoh what the Israelites want to sacrifice in the desert,[34] and in fact the freed Israelites *do* promptly offer *'olot*—to the golden calf![35] The *'olah* is especially used on public occasions to inaugurate a covenant,[36] to celebrate a festival,[37] or to pray for a military victory.[38]

The altar in front of the tabernacle was used for all kinds of animal sacrifices; remember that this is the outermost altar where the blood of the *chatta't* goes, the first stage of penetration of the miasma of sin into the sanctuary. But it's sometimes referred to as the "altar of the *'olah*,"[39] as though the *'olah* can serve as a kind of shorthand for sacrifices in general.

The term *'olah* is even used for foreign sacrifices. Jethro the Midianite, Moses' father-in-law, offers an *'olah*;[40] he's sacrificing to the Lord, but at a point in the story where God hasn't given any instructions about sacrifices yet. Since Jethro is described as a priest,[41] we're probably supposed to understand that Jethro was already familiar with the practice from his own culture. Similarly, the story of Job is set in a pre-Sinai era, but we see Job

---

31. Morales, *Who Shall Ascend?*, 122.
32. Gen 8:20.
33. Gen 22.
34. Exod 10:25.
35. Exod 32:4–6.
36. Exod 24:5–8.
37. Lev 23:12, 18.
38. 1 Sam 7:9–10.
39. Exod 30:28; 31:9; 35:16; 38:1; 40:6, 10, 29; Lev 4:7, 10, 18, 25, 30, 34.
40. Exod 18:12.
41. Exod 18:1.

offering ʿolot on behalf of his children.[42] The Moabite king Balak sacrifices ʿolot to try to convince the divine powers to produce omens against the Israelites,[43] and the later Moabite king Mesha offers his own son as an ʿolah.[44] Other passages describe Israelites offering ʿolot to Baal.[45] All this suggests either that ʿolah also functioned as a general term for all kinds of sacrifices, or that the Israelites believed the ritual of the ʿolah was a kind of prototype of sacrifices in general, or possibly some combination of the two.

The details of the ritual procedure for the ʿolah have proven to be fertile ground for symbolic or allegorical interpretations. The animal has to be male;[46] Philo, in classic Philonic fashion, explains that the male sex is associated with superior things: dominion, intellect, and reason.[47] (This is a good time to remind the reader that one purpose of this book is to show the rich variety of ways commentators have understood sacrifice, and that I don't necessarily endorse every interpretation described here!)

After the animal is killed, its skin is removed;[48] the skin is the only part that isn't burned, and it belongs to the priests. Writing in the twelfth century, Ralph of Flaix sees a spiritual meaning here: "We remove the skin of the sacrifice when we, not content with the superficial in life, see past the things which are only good to look at and see the hidden vices."[49] The priests burn wood on the altar and arrange the animal, in pieces, on the wood. Hertz makes the striking observation that this arrangement means the fire would pass between the pieces of the sacrifice, like the torch that God sent between the pieces of Abraham's offering when he made a covenant with him.[50] Ralph of Flaix interprets the wood as "the virtuous thinking which encourages the Holy Spirit to blaze so that doing good becomes a pleasure."[51] The entrails and legs of the animal are washed; for Philo, washing the entrails means that we should purify ourselves from evil

---

42. Job 1:5.
43. Num 23:15.
44. 2 Kgs 3:27.
45. 2 Kgs 10:24; Jer 19:5.
46. Lev 1:3.
47. Philo, *Spec.* 1.200–201.
48. Lev 1:6.
49. Ralph of Flaix, *Leviticum Libri*, 3; quoted in Elliott, *Engaging Leviticus*, 7.
50. Gen 15:9–21; Hertz, *Pentateuch and Haftorahs*, 412.
51. Ralph of Flaix, *Leviticum Libri*, 3; quoted in Elliott, *Engaging Leviticus*, 7.

desires such as drunkenness, and washing the feet means that "we must no longer walk upon the earth, but soar aloft and traverse the air."[52]

The first chapter of Leviticus describes three types of *'olah*, in descending order of cost: a bull, a sheep or goat, and a bird. This kind of sliding scale shows up frequently in the sacrificial regulations; many commentators have pointed out that this pattern makes sacrifice accessible to everyone, even those who can't afford an expensive animal. For the *'olah* with birds, Nachmanides sees a special significance in which species are allowed: doves, because they're faithful to their mates, just as Israel must be faithful to God; or pigeons, who are *not* faithful as adults, and therefore must be offered while they're still young.[53]

Pulling back from the details, the general picture of the *'olah* as a whole offering to God seems pretty clear. Every other sacrifice is partly eaten by the priests or the offerer (except for certain instances of the *chatta't*). Only the *'olah* is entirely burned; no human being benefits from its meat. Moreover, the image of the smoke going up to God is an excellent way to represent what's going on in *all* sacrifices: worshippers drawing near to God. This idea is deeply embedded in the laws themselves; one of the technical terms in the legal material for offering a sacrifice is a verb that literally means "bring near." It's easy to see why many ancient people (most likely including some Israelites) believed that burnt offerings literally transferred the animal from the human sphere to the divine one.

There's not much in the New Testament that explicitly links Jesus with the *'olah*, as opposed to other types of sacrifice. But insofar as the *'olah* represents a complete self-giving to God, we absolutely see Jesus doing what the *'olah* points toward: he submits to the will of God,[54] gives up everything he is and has,[55] and ultimately offers the "sacrifice of himself."[56] And the death of Jesus accomplishes the "bringing near" that was the goal of all sacrifice:

> Therefore, brethren, since we have confidence to enter the sanctuary by the blood of Jesus, by the new and living way which he opened for us through the curtain, that is, through his flesh, and

---

52. Philo, *Spec.* 1.206–7 (Yonge).
53. Nachmanides, *Leviticus* 1:14.
54. Luke 22:42; John 8:28.
55. Phil 2:6–8.
56. Heb 9:26.

since we have a great priest over the house of God, *let us draw near with a true heart in full assurance of faith....*[57]

The *shelamim*: A shared meal

The fourth major type of sacrifice is the *shelamim*, detailed in Leviticus 3. (The Hebrew word is grammatically plural, but it's used even when the context makes it clear that there was only one sacrifice.[58] The singular form *shelem* is extremely rare;[59] modern English commentators often just use *shelamim*.) If you notice that the name of this sacrifice shares a root with *shalom*, then you'll understand why this sacrifice has traditionally been translated as the "peace offering" (KJV). The *shlm* root, of course, has connotations that go beyond English "peace," including "wholeness" and "completeness," which is what the NRSV tries to capture in its translation "sacrifice of well-being." The rabbis of the Second Temple period associated the *shelamim* with the full range of these meanings: "Whoever brings a sacrifice in the category of peace-offerings [*shelamim*] brings peace to the world."[60] "He who is at peace [and whole in body and soul] may bring an offering in the status of peace-offerings [*shelamim*]."[61]

An Akkadian word derived from the same etymologically related root, *shulmanu*, means "gift"—usually to a king or some other high-ranking official, but sometimes to a god. Baruch Levine, drawing on this parallel and also noting the use of *shalom* as a verbal greeting in Hebrew, suggests translating this sacrifice as the "sacred gift of greeting."[62] Even in a religious context, though, an Akkadian *shulmanu* for a god typically involves silver or gold rather than animal sacrifice.[63] Moreover, Old Testament Hebrew has a word that corresponds to *shulmanu*, and *shelamim* isn't it.[64] The *shelamim* of the Old Testament doesn't look like the Akkadian gift at all; in fact, only a small part of the animal is burned on the altar: the kidneys, part of the

---

57. Heb 10:19–22a, RSV, emphasis added.
58. Num 6:14.
59. Amos 5:22.
60. *Sifra*, Nedavah 16.1 (Neusner).
61. *Sifra*, Nedavah 16.2 (Neusner).
62. Levine, *Leviticus*, 15.
63. *CAD* 17.3.244–7.
64. BDB 1024.

liver, and the fat around them.[65] The text of Leviticus 3 doesn't say explicitly what happens to the rest of the animal, but plenty of other passages make it clear: part of it goes to the priest,[66] and then the worshipper and his or her guests eat the sacrifice in a feast of celebration.[67]

If I bring a sacrifice and then I throw a party for my friends and family where we eat most of the meat, how can we call that a sacrifice at all? Once again, we're seeing that sacrifices are just as much for the benefit of the worshipper as they are for God. The *shelamim* emphasizes the horizontal relationships among people that we saw with the *'asham*, plus the drawing near to God that we saw with the *'olah*. The rabbis recognized the fundamentally relational nature of the *shelamim*:

> Peace-offerings [*shelamim*] are so called because all are at peace, each sharing in them. Parts of them, the blood and the limbs, are for the altar, part, the breast and the thigh, for the priests, part, the hide and the meat, for the owner.[68]

The NIV honors this focus on sharing when it translates the *shelamim* as the "fellowship offering."

In fact, most of the sacrificial meals we see in the Old Testament are probably *shelamim*: Elkanah, Samuel, and Adonijah all have feasts associated with sacrifices.[69] The word used in these passages is *zevach*, a general term for sacrifice that literally means "slaughter," or its related verb—but here and in many other passages, *zevach* seems to be short for *zevach shelamim* (the "*shelamim* sacrifice"). When you gather at the sanctuary for a sacrifice, everyone knows that after the *'olah* you're going to offer a *shelamim* to close out the celebration with a meal.[70] (Or, as in some of the stories just mentioned, you might gather to offer *only* a *shelamim*, especially for local celebrations too small to support an expensive *'olah*.)

Christian interpreters up through the medieval period haven't had much to say about the *shelamim*, other than to observe that burning the inner fat of the animal on the altar suggests that we should offer our

---

65. Lev 3:3–5, 9–11, 14–16.
66. Lev 7:31–36.
67. Lev 7:11–21; Deut 12:6–7; 27:7; 2 Sam 6:18–19; 1 Kgs 3:15.
68. *Sifra*, Nedavah 16.2 (Neusner).
69. 1 Sam 1:3–7; 9:11–24; 1 Kgs 1:9, 41.
70. Deut 12:6; 1 Kgs 8:64.

thoughts and desires to God.[71] I find this surprising, because there's a beautiful—and extremely obvious—comparison just waiting to be made between the *shelamim* and the Lord's supper. Here we have a shared meal where worshippers come together to have fellowship with each other and with God, where Jesus himself is the sacrifice whose body is represented by the communion bread.[72]

This doesn't mean the Lord's supper was directly modeled on the *shelamim*; it wasn't. The most striking difference is that Leviticus prohibits consuming the blood of the *shelamim*,[73] whereas the cup that represents Jesus' blood is just as important as the bread.[74] But it's fair to say that God gave his people gifts through the *shelamim*, and he continues to give those same gifts through the Lord's supper. In the thirteenth century, Hugh of St. Cher suggested that in the *shelamim* God himself is both the offerer and priest who brings peace to worshippers;[75] it's hard to imagine a better summary of Jesus' priestly role as described in Hebrews. The Septuagint, the Greek translation of the Old Testament in popular use during the New Testament period, translates the *shelamim* as the "sacrifice of salvation;" could anything be more appropriate for God's people gathering to remember the "pioneer of their salvation"?[76]

Other sacrifices

I said earlier that the first part of Leviticus describes four major types of sacrifices. Actually, this isn't quite true; chapter 2—right after the *'olah*—presents one more type, the *minchah*. So why not include the *minchah* in a list of *five* major sacrifices? After all, the traditional chapter divisions suggest a status for the *minchah* equal with the others.

A five-fold classification is perfectly reasonable. But when we look at the occasions when the *minchah* is offered, it seems less like its own sacrifice and more like an accompaniment to, or a variant of, other sacrifices. *Minchah* is a word that means "gift," and it can be used for sacrifices in

---

71. Elliott, *Engaging Leviticus*, 22–26.
72. Matt 26:26 // Mark 14:22 // Luke 22:19; 1 Cor 11:23–24.
73. Lev 3:2, 8, 13, 17.
74. Matt 26:27 // Mark 14:23 // Luke 22:20; 1 Cor 11:25.
75. Hugh of St. Cher, *In Libros*, 104.
76. Heb 2:10.

general (e.g., both Cain's and Abel's offerings[77]). But as a technical term it refers to offerings of grain, not animals—hence the translation "grain offering" or "cereal offering." The fact that it's ordered right after the *'olah* is important: remember that chapter 1 lists three types of animals for the *'olah*, from most expensive to least expensive (bull, sheep or goat, bird). In this context, the *minchah* looks like an even more accessible option for the *'olah*; if the worshipper can't afford a bird, he or she can surely afford some grain. Both Jewish and Christian commentators have a long history of interpreting the *minchah* in exactly this way.[78] Christian interpreters often compare this offering to the way Jesus praised the poor widow who came to the temple and offered "all she had to live on,"[79] and plenty of Jewish writers make the same point that God is happy to accept inexpensive offerings from sincere worshippers:

> But [God] delights in minds which love God, and in men who practice holiness, from whom he gladly receives cakes and barley, and the very cheapest things, as if they were the most valuable in preference to such as are most costly.[80]

So the *minchah* finishes the sliding scale of the *'olah*; it throws open wide the entrance to the sanctuary and invites everyone to come experience the presence of God through sacrifice.

The *minchah* also accompanies other offerings. There are regulations in Numbers, for example, that specify how much grain (plus oil and wine to go with it) should be offered along with animals of various types: more for a larger animal, and less for a smaller.[81] Even if it isn't explicitly designated as an add-on to some other sacrifice, ritual instructions that call for the *minchah* usually include it as one of several sacrifices to be offered on the same occasion.[82]

Outside the sanctuary, though, it was a different story. There's evidence that the *minchah* was offered in places other than the official altar, and that—in contrast to all the other sacrifices—the temple authorities were

---

77. Gen 4:3–4.
78. Milgrom, *Leviticus 1–16*, 195–96; Elliott, *Engaging Leviticus*, 18.
79. Mark 12:41–44 // Luke 21:1–4.
80. Philo, *Spec.* 1.271 (Yonge).
81. Num 15:1–10.
82. Num 6:13–15.

Not All Sacrifices Are about Sin

okay with this.[83] There was a Jewish community in the Egyptian fortress settlement at Elephantine, on the Nile at the southern border of Egypt, who had their own temple. (This is already pretty remarkable, given how central the Jerusalem temple was to Israel and Judah!) The Elephantine temple was eventually destroyed too, over a century after the first temple in Jerusalem was, apparently in a local religious conflict. Shortly thereafter, the priests wrote to the authorities in Persian-occupied Judea asking for permission to rebuild it:

> [L]et a letter be sent from you to them concerning the temple of the God Ya'u [Yahweh] to build it in the fortress of Yeb [Elephantine] as it was built before, and they shall offer the meal-offering [Aramaic equivalent of *minchah*] and incense and sacrifice [Aramaic equivalent of *'olah*] on the altar of the God Ya'u on your behalf, and we will pray for you at all times. . . .[84]

The answer was "yes," but only for the *minchah* and incense; apparently, the religious leaders in Jerusalem drew the line at the *'olah*. Later rabbis agreed that the *minchah* could be offered anywhere, citing the prophet Malachi:

> For from the rising of the sun to its setting my name is great among the nations, and *in every place* incense is offered to my name, and a pure offering [*minchah*]; for my name is great among the nations, says the LORD of hosts.[85]

Once again, the *minchah* expands the boundaries of sacrifice. It's accessible to all worshippers, regardless of class and regardless of geography. It's a beautiful thing when God's people gather at the sanctuary to worship together, but the *minchah* shows that it's *also* a beautiful thing when they carry that worshipping spirit back to their home communities.

There are several other named sacrifices that are—usually—subtypes of the main four. Leviticus 7 lists three specific occasions for bringing a *shelamim*, each with its own name: an offering of thanksgiving (*todah*), an offering to fulfill a vow (*neder*), and an offering of spontaneous rejoicing (a "freewill" offering, *nedavah*).[86] In fact, the *shelamim* itself is never mentioned in the psalms; all the references to sacrifice that we saw in chapter 3

---

83. Milgrom, *Leviticus 1–16*, 199–200.
84. Cowley, *Aramaic Papyri*, 114.
85. Mal 1:11, emphasis added.
86. Lev 7:11–18.

use one of these more specific terms, or name some other kind of sacrifice altogether.

One particular sacrifice was offered twice every day, a lamb *'olah* and its accompanying *minchah*:[87] once in the morning and once in the evening. This *tamid*, as it was later known (the "continual" offering), is just one of lots of ways the sanctuary reflects God's good ordering of creation. There's a long strand of Jewish interpretive tradition that associates the structure of the sanctuary, or the clothing of the high priest, with the structure of the universe—especially the sun, moon, stars, and other astronomical entities.[88] The *tamid* echoes the rhythm of creation described in Genesis 1: evening and morning, evening and morning, day in and day out.

A few other occasion-specific sacrifices don't fit neatly into one of the main four categories, such as the ram that's sacrificed for the ordination of a priest.[89] Probably the most notable example is the Passover sacrifice. It's most similar to the *shelamim* (because worshippers eat it in family groups), but it's never explicitly called a *shelamim* in the Old Testament; this sacrifice is something slightly different.

This bewildering variety of sacrifices—the types of offering, the animals and plants that could be brought, the occasions when people brought them—should make us hesitate before we try to pin down the one or two "real" meanings of sacrifice. We can try to box sacrifice in, to tame it with neat categories; but, as an expression of the rich relationship between God and his people, it will keep leaking out in unexpected ways. Sacrifice isn't the only way worshippers can relate to God; Judaism thrives even without a temple. But many people have found it to be a deeply meaningful part of their life with God. If we want to enter into the world of scripture, we have to reckon with sacrifice in all its messiness and complexity.

Covering, wiping, and atonement

There's one more technical term we need to deal with before we move on from sacrifices. The rituals of the *'olah*,[90] the *chatta't*,[91] and the *'asham*[92] are

87. Exod 29:38–42; Num 28:3–8.
88. Klawans, *Symbolism and Supersessionism*, 113–28.
89. Exod 29:19–27; Lev 8:22–36.
90. Lev 1:4.
91. Lev 4:20, 26, 31, 35.
92. Lev 6:7.

Not All Sacrifices Are about Sin

all said to "make atonement," and this is (of course) a major part of the Day of Atonement.[93] But what exactly does that mean?

It turns out that the English word "atonement" isn't terribly helpful in illuminating what's going on here, especially since it's so closely associated with Christian theological understandings of the death of Jesus. It conveys the idea of God and his people becoming "at one," but beyond that there's a lot of room for different interpretations of the specifics of how this happens. The Hebrew verb is *kipper*—hence Yom Kippur, the Day of Atonement. This verb is connected with three different fields of meaning (or possibly two, depending on how you count), with distinct implications for how we understand what these sacrifices are doing.

The first meaning is "cover," inferred from a possibly related Arabic root.[94] The literal cover of the ark of the covenant, often translated "mercy seat," is the *kapporet*,[95] which could lend support to the idea that *kipper* is associated with "covering." On this understanding, then, one of the fundamental functions of sacrifice is that it "covers over" something—presumably, human sin. This interpretation is fine as far as it goes, and it has a strong affinity with penal substitutionary theories: we could say that the death of the animal "covers" the guilt of the person, that the animal gets between a wrathful God and a sinful human in order to shield the human from the punishment he deserves. But, as we saw in chapter 3, sacrifice in general in the Old Testament just doesn't seem to use a penal substitutionary model. We could take one *possible* meaning of *kipper*, plus a theory about how Jesus' death works, and project that back onto the whole sacrificial system—but it feels like a stretch.

The second meaning is, roughly, "ransom." This interpretation has plenty of support in the Old Testament; the noun *kopher* has exactly this meaning. For example, if a man owns an ox that's known to be dangerous, and the ox kills someone, he can avoid the death penalty by paying a ransom—a *kopher*.[96] And in non-ritual contexts, the verb *kipper* can mean "pay a *kopher*." When Jacob is about to see his brother Esau for the first time in twenty years, and he's worried that Esau is still angry about being cheated

---

93. Lev 16:6, 10–11, 16–18, 20, 24, 27, 30, 32–34.
94. BDB 497.
95. Exod 25:17–22.
96. Exod 21:28–30.

out of his inheritance, he sends a gift with the thought, "I may appease [*kipper*] him with the present that goes ahead of me."[97]

We could see the "ransom" meaning as related to the "cover" meaning; the payment "covers over" the guilt of the person who did wrong. Sometimes *kipper* has a more abstract meaning, where a literal ransom payment isn't necessarily involved. When Isaiah has a vision of God on his throne, a heavenly creature "blots out" (*kipper*) Isaiah's sin by touching his lips with a hot coal taken from the altar.[98] And so *kipper* sometimes has the more general meaning "expiate" ("deal with sin") or "propitiate" ("make someone less angry"). The translators of the Septuagint leaned towards the second option; they translated *kipper*, especially in the context of sacrifices, with *hilaskomai*, a Greek verb that originally had strong "propitiation" connotations. But, like *kipper*, this verb doesn't have to imply anger; it can just mean that the god is gracious.[99] (Similarly, in the Old Testament, *kipper* can be used with God as the subject, meaning simply "forgive."[100])

Like the "cover" meaning, the "ransom" meaning has affinities with penal substitution.[101] But although the "ransom" idea is definitely substitutionary, it's not necessarily penal. When Jacob sends a gift of goats and other animals to Esau, the point isn't exactly to punish himself for having hurt Esau—if that were the goal, then presumably Jacob could have accomplished the same thing by, say, driving the animals over a cliff. ("Look! I just destroyed a bunch of my property. See how sorry I am?") It's hard to imagine that Esau would have been impressed by this. Instead, it's the *relational* aspect that matters here; Jacob gives a gift *to Esau*, symbolically offering repayment for what he stole. In other words, to the extent that a ransom is penal, it's not substitutionary (Jacob's payment hurts him, not the animals); to the extent that it's substitutionary, it's not penal. This is even more true of ransom payments that involve money; sure, the money in a sense takes the place of the person's life, but not because we're punishing the money instead of the person.

As *kipper* develops a more abstract meaning, even the substitutionary idea starts to fall away. The hot coal that touches Isaiah's lips in the

---

97. Gen 32:20.
98. Isa 6:6.
99. Büchsel, "ἱλάσκομαι, ἱλασμός B–E," 314.
100. Ps 65:3.
101. Kiuchi, *Leviticus*, 46–47, 56–57, 61, 96, 322; Levine, *Leviticus*, 21–22, 115–16; Wenham, *Leviticus*, 28–29, 59–61.

vision doesn't look like a punishment ("You deserve to die, but how about a painful burn instead?"), and it looks even less like substitution (since Isaiah is the only person involved). In fact, what Isaiah's vision most resembles is the cleansing of the *chatta't*. After all, the coal incident is prompted by Isaiah himself with explicit reference to pollution: "Woe is me! I am lost, for I am a man of *unclean lips*, and I live among a people of *unclean lips*; yet my eyes have seen the King, the Lord of hosts!"[102]

This brings us to the third possible meaning of *kipper*: "wipe." Akkadian has a related word with this meaning;[103] it's the word that describes what the priest does with the ram's body in the Akitu festival we saw in chapter 4. The idea of wiping fits perfectly with the cleansing blood of the *chatta't*, which the priest puts on the altar in order to purify it. (It's even possible that the "cover" and "wipe" meanings are related after all: "wipe on" versus "wipe off."[104]) In sacrificial contexts, the verb *kipper* often appears with other verbs that have a "cleansing" or "purifying" meaning. Milgrom, who adopts this meaning, translates *kipper* as "purge" and the Day of Atonement as the "Day of Purgation."[105]

It's not possible to be certain how ancient Israelites, or Jews in the Second Temple period, understood *kipper*—if there was even unanimity in the first place! And whatever the etymological source of the word is, it's clear that in ritual texts such as Leviticus the word has acquired a technical meaning. It describes what the sacrifice accomplishes (setting people right with God), not necessarily a single mechanism by which that happens. I believe this is why *kipper* is occasionally associated with the *'olah*,[106] even though that sacrifice's ransoming and cleansing themes are marginal at best; with incense,[107] prayer,[108] treasure,[109] and good deeds,[110] which aren't animal sacrifices at all; and with sacrifices that deal with ritual impurity that wasn't caused by sin in the first place.[111]

---

102. Isa 6:5, emphasis added.
103. Wright, *Disposal of Impurity*, 291–99.
104. Milgrom, *Leviticus 1–16*, 1080.
105. Milgrom, *Leviticus 1–16*, 1009–84.
106. Lev 1:4.
107. Num 16:47.
108. Exod 32:30–32.
109. Num 31:50.
110. Prov 16:6.
111. Lev 12:7–8; 14:18–31; 15:15, 30.

In fact, we've come full circle: as long as we avoid attributing full-fledged Christian theology to ancient Jewish priests, I think "make atonement" is actually a pretty decent translation of *kipper*. It gets at the core of the matter without committing to a particular theory of how sacrifices work; and as we've seen, sacrifice is a lot of things, not just one thing. God's relationship with his people is rich and multifaceted, and so is the vocabulary we use to describe how that relationship is set right.

Behold the lamb of God

The gospel of John reports that one day John the Baptist saw Jesus and said, "Here is the Lamb of God who takes away the sin of the world!"[112] Sacrifices were an important way Jews dealt with sin, and lambs were a common sacrificial animal—so it sounds like John is talking about Jesus as a sacrifice. Now that we've looked at so many types of sacrifices, and in such great detail, we should be able to get a deeper insight into John's statement by identifying what kind of sacrifice he was talking about. Right?

Well, no. If we're looking for a sacrifice that takes away sin, the obvious one is the *chatta't*. But there's a problem: even though a sheep was an option,[113] the *chatta't* was overwhelmingly associated with goats. Almost every prescription for what animal to offer as a *chatta't* on some particular occasion specifies a goat,[114] and almost every story of someone offering a *chatta't* describes a goat.[115] We occasionally hear of a bull,[116] *but never a lamb*. If John had wanted to compare Jesus to a *chatta't*, he should have said, "Here is the Goat of God who takes away the sin of the world!"

It's not wrong to compare Jesus to a *chatta't*; as we've already seen, the New Testament writers talk about how Jesus' blood washes us clean, so the comparison is a deeply scriptural one. I'm just not convinced that John intended to invoke the *chatta't* here. But if not the *chatta't*, what else could he have meant? The *'olah* isn't usually a sheep either; as with the *chatta't*, a sheep is possible,[117] but other animals are much more common. The exception is the twice-daily *tamid*, which is a lamb, but the Old Testament never

---

112. John 1:29.
113. Lev 4:32.
114. Lev 16:9; 23:19; Num 28:15, 22; 29:5, 11, 16–38.
115. Lev 9:15; Num 7; 2 Chr 29:21–24; Ezra 6:17; 8:35.
116. Exod 29:10–14; Lev 8:2; 16:3; Num 8:8.
117. Lev 1:10.

says anything about the *tamid* taking away sin. Similarly, the *shelamim* could be a sheep, and the Passover sacrifice is always a lamb, but those sacrifices aren't about sin either. Or maybe John isn't referring to a sacrifice after all; maybe he means the suffering servant of Isaiah ("like a lamb that is led to the slaughter"[118]) or the conquering lamb that was familiar from Jewish apocalyptic literature.[119]

All these interpretations, and more, have been proposed by Christian writers.[120] The proposal I find most persuasive is that John the Baptist is, in fact, referring to the Passover lamb. As articulated by N. T. Wright, this new lamb of God takes away sin—not because the original Passover lamb did this, but because the Jewish people of the time saw themselves in need of a new exodus, a new deliverance from slavery (not least from the occupying Roman powers), and this would require dealing with the sin that resulted in their exile and bondage in the first place.[121] The Passover theme shows up everywhere in the New Testament, especially in the gospel of John: Jesus was crucified at Passover time and, like the Passover lamb, his bones weren't broken.[122] So seeing a Passover reference here too doesn't require any great stretch of the imagination.

This image—Jesus, the lamb of God, who takes away the sin of the world—drives home the point of this chapter. The Passover sacrifice is deeply embedded in the story of redemption history, but it's fair to suggest that it was possible for John to relate Passover to sin because there were *other* sacrifices that *did* have this focus. All the different types of offerings help us name aspects of life with God in rich and specific ways, but God isn't limited by the old categories. God's salvation bursts apart the puzzle pieces, only to put them back together again in fresh combinations. God's love overflows our cups and refills them with something new. And so, although it's valuable to point out how particular sacrifices allowed worshippers to relate to God in specific ways, we shouldn't expect God to sit tamely in those boxes. Already in the Old Testament, we see people joyfully approaching God through sacrifice, but not *only* through sacrifice. For millennia, God's faithful people have found diverse ways to encounter the living God who is always doing a new thing.

118. Isa 53:7.
119. 1 En. 90:6–12; Rev 5:6.
120. Brown, *John 1-12*, 58–63.
121. Wright, *Revolution*, 169–94.
122. Exod 12:46; John 19:31–33.

6

Not All Dirt Is Sin

I LOVE TACOS! The problem is that I'm not very good at eating them. I get filling all over my mouth and hands, and by the time I'm done I've spilled half of it on my plate. Just about every taco I eat is followed immediately by a trip to the sink for a thorough hand-washing. (Followed by attacking the stray filling with a fork—and then, sometimes, by another taco.)

So, when I eat tacos, I know I'm going to have to clean up afterwards. Definitely my hands, usually my face, often the table, and sometimes even my pants if I was especially uncoordinated that day. This is all fine; it's just part of the experience, and I know to expect it. Here's the important thing: *cleaning up is not a punishment for eating tacos*. Eating tacos is a *good* thing; it's just intrinsically messy, so of course I have to deal with the aftermath.

We've spent a fair amount of time exploring how Old Testament theology imagines sin as a kind of pollution, and how sacrifices like the *chatta't* deal with sin by cleansing or purifying what it's polluted. The theme of this chapter is that we can't apply this line of thinking to every passage in the Old Testament that talks about impurity. The ritual regulations have a lot to say about impurity in contexts that have nothing to do with sin. In short: *sin is like dirt, but not all dirt is sin*.

Numbers 19 is a good example of this. The first part of the chapter describes the procedure for making ritual cleansing water, using the ashes of a red cow specially prepared by the priests. Then we learn what this water is for:

Not All Dirt Is Sin

> Those who touch the dead body of any human being shall be unclean seven days. They shall purify themselves with the water on the third day and on the seventh day, and so be clean; but if they do not purify themselves on the third day and on the seventh day, they will not become clean. All who touch a corpse, the body of a human being who has died, and do not purify themselves, defile the tabernacle of the Lord; such persons shall be cut off from Israel. Since the water for cleansing was not dashed on them, they remain unclean; their uncleanness is still on them.[1]

For a long time, my first instinct when I read this passage was to interpret it as a prohibition, combined with the punishment for violating that prohibition: "Do not touch a dead body. If you do, your punishment is that you must purify yourself." But this reading invents a punishment where none is intended; as we'll soon see, burying the dead was *not* prohibited, and in fact it was considered a righteous act. Purification after touching a corpse is no more a punishment than washing your hands after a messy meal.

That's not to say that "neutral" dirt can't also involve wrongdoing. If my children have spaghetti sauce all over their hands and faces after dinner, that's fine. But if they go wallow on the couch before washing up, that is most definitely *not* fine. It's okay to drop crumbs on the floor, but it's not okay to leave them there all night so they attract ants. If the kids accidentally knock over a cup of milk, that's understandable; but if they knock over a cup that was carelessly left too close to the edge of the table, despite repeated warnings, they will get a serious talking-to.

In other words, this kind of dirt isn't a problem by itself. Rather, the problem is creating extra dirt through carelessness, or not cleaning up promptly, or bringing the dirt into contact with things that deserve special attention. This is precisely what's happening in the Numbers passage: it *does* describe a punishment (being "cut off from Israel"), but the context makes it clear that this punishment is for those who neglect the purification ritual: "the water of cleansing was not dashed on them."

But when we hear words like "clean" and "unclean," or "pure" and "impure," it's hard to avoid thinking about morality too; impurity and wrongdoing are closely associated in human psychology.[2] So it's going to take a lot of effort to start undoing some of those associations. Some scholars avoid words like "unclean" or "impure" altogether and translate the Hebrew

---

1. Num 19:11–13.
2. Beck, *Unclean*, 33–50.

term *tame'* ("unclean/impure") as "taboo" or "restricted"[3]—because, as we'll see, the main consequence of ritual impurity is that the impure person can't go near holy things. I appreciate this line of thinking; the link between impurity and sin runs deep, and to see things any other way we're going to need all the help we can get. But Hebrew *tame'* (and *tahor*, "clean/pure") *do* have more generic purity meanings too: the Old Testament writers can talk about a "pure heart"[4] or an "unclean spirit"[5] using the same vocabulary. And the early translators who produced the Greek version of the Old Testament known as the Septuagint agreed; they chose Greek words with strong purity meanings to translate *tame'* and *tahor*. So it's not illegitimate to connect these terms to purity; in fact, it's deeply scriptural.

Another argument against using "un/clean" or "im/pure" as English translations is that *tame'* and *tahor* aren't related: morphologically, *tame'* isn't "un-*tahor*;" it's a separate root altogether. Personally, I don't find this argument convincing. It's a perfectly normal thing for languages to denote opposites with unrelated words: think "hot/cold" or "long/short." English speakers recognize that these words refer to opposite ends of a scale; we don't need "hot/unhot" or "long/unlong" to see the connection. All in all, "un/clean" and "im/pure" do a pretty decent job of conveying what they need to convey. Not perfect—after all, we're about to spend a whole chapter trying to weaken the connection between impurity and sin—but good enough for now. I'll mostly use "pure" and "impure," but we can expect to see "clean" and "unclean" pop up from time to time as well.

This chapter explores types of impurity that are *not* sinful. Many commentators, especially Christian ones, have tended to conflate impurity language around sin with other nonsinful impurities—and to exaggerate the consequences of nonsinful impurity. We'll devote some extra time to looking at sources of impurity that are particularly troubling to many modern readers: menstruation and childbirth. This chapter is essentially negative, dispelling myths about what impurity was and how it worked. A more constructive approach (what's the point of all this, anyway?) will have to wait until chapter 7.

---

3. Gafney, *Womanist Midrash*, 109–12.
4. Ps 51:10; Prov 22:11.
5. Zech 13:2.

Not All Dirt Is Sin

Ritual impurity versus moral impurity

A close reading of the Old Testament reveals two impurity systems that are, essentially, independent of each other;[6] the distinction is honored in most postbiblical literature too.[7] Jonathan Klawans calls these systems "moral impurity" and "ritual impurity."[8] "Moral impurity" is the defilement that results from sin, the kind we saw in chapter 4. "Ritual impurity" is generally nonsinful and has the primary effect of regulating access to the sanctuary.

This terminology for these systems isn't perfect. For one thing, it's false to say that moral impurity doesn't have ritual implications; the rituals of the *chatta't*, the *'asham*, and the Day of Atonement are all closely related to moral impurity. Conversely, ritual impurity *can* involve ethics—for the reasons hinted at above, and for symbolic reasons that we'll explore further in chapter 7. We could try other words; Tikva Frymer-Kensky, for example, suggests "pollution beliefs" and "danger beliefs."[9] But using "ritual impurity" and "moral impurity" preserves the fact that the two systems are related, and these terms still do a pretty good job of getting at a basic distinction between them: moral impurity is the result of *immoral actions* by people, whereas ritual impurity involves morally neutral actions or situations that have *ritual implications*.

There are several strands of evidence that the Old Testament treats ritual impurity and moral impurity as different things. One, which we won't discuss here, is that scripture uses slightly different vocabulary for the two systems: some terms overlap, but others are used *only* for moral impurity.[10] More convincing is that ritual impurity and moral impurity differ in what causes impurity in the first place, how that impurity is transmitted, and what its consequences are.

There are three major sources of ritual impurity in the Old Testament: human corpses; certain skin conditions, plus analogous mildew on fabrics and walls; and genital emissions, including sex and childbirth. (The dietary laws, which designate certain animals as unclean, have something like an intermediate status; we'll reserve discussion of those for chapter 8. There are also a few minor cases where ritual impurity is a byproduct of some other

---

6. Frymer-Kensky, "Pollution," 399–414.
7. Klawans, *Impurity and Sin*.
8. Klawans, *Impurity and Sin*, 22–23.
9. Frymer-Kensky, "Pollution," 404.
10. Klawans, *Impurity and Sin*, 26–28, 37.

ritual procedure.[11]) A person with any of these three conditions can often make other people impure by touching them, and sometimes—depending on the specific type of impurity and other details of the circumstances—can render objects impure, and even people who touch those objects, either by direct contact or by sharing an enclosed space. *None of these three conditions is inherently sinful.* Having a skin disease isn't sinful; neither is menstruating or having a discharge from your penis. And, as noted above, some of these conditions are the direct result of *good* actions: caring for the dead is good and necessary, and it's hard to imagine how the Israelites could fulfill God's command to "be fruitful and multiply"[12] without having sex or giving birth.

All this is very different from the examples in chapter 4 where scripture discusses moral impurity. The most obvious difference is that the actions that cause moral impurity are, well, sins. Scripture as a whole makes it perfectly clear that idolatry, murder, and so on are wrong. But it's not just the source of the impurity; these two systems also pollute in different ways. Moral impurity, as we saw, is like an aerial miasma that pollutes the sanctuary pretty much automatically. This pollution happens at a distance; the altar needs to be purified, even though the sinner most likely hasn't been anywhere near the altar until coming to offer the *chatta't*. But moral impurity is *not* transmitted by direct contact; there are no laws, for example, that you become impure if you touch a murderer or sit on the same chair as an idolater. There's plenty of advice against associating too closely with immoral people, because you might start imitating their behavior—"Happy are those who do not . . . take the path that sinners tread, or sit in the seat of scoffers"[13]—but that's different from saying that being near a sinful person makes you ritually impure.

By contrast, ritual impurity definitely pollutes by contact, but it doesn't necessarily pollute the sanctuary from a distance. (The Numbers passage above states that someone who neglects to purify himself after touching a corpse will pollute the sanctuary, but it's not clear that the same is true for someone who purifies himself promptly. It's the difference between cleaning up crumbs from the floor right away versus leaving them out to attract ants.) Rather, the concern with ritual impurity is that *the impure person must not physically approach the sanctuary or holy things.* A person who is

11. Num 19:2–10, 19–21.
12. Gen 1:28; 9:1; 35:11.
13. Ps 1:1.

ritually impure can't eat a *shelamim*[14] or bring a tithe;[15] priests have to be especially careful not to carry out their duties or eat holy food while they're impure.[16]

Two examples help make the difference clear. First, Numbers 5 describes an elaborate ritual for a woman suspected of adultery. The whole procedure is fascinating (and not a little scary), but what's important to notice here is that the text explicitly says the ritual takes place *at the tabernacle*.[17] In other words, we have a woman who may well have sinned, and she physically comes right up to the altar. Such a thing would be unthinkable if the question were whether the woman is ritually impure; a potentially impure person wouldn't go anywhere near the sanctuary. But for a person who is (or might be) *morally* impure, approaching the sanctuary is fine. The ritually impure person pollutes the sanctuary, but the morally impure person doesn't. Or, more precisely: if the woman really has sinned, then she has *already* polluted the sanctuary (morally); coming to the altar doesn't make things any worse than they already are. But a ritually impure person *doesn't* pollute the sanctuary from a distance; only physically approaching would be a problem.

The second example is a legend set in the time of the second temple, told a century or two after the temple was destroyed. In this story, one priest stabs another at the altar; the authorities react with distress because a human corpse conveys an extremely serious ritual impurity. While everyone is panicking, the father of the priest who was stabbed steps in to save the day by pointing out that his son isn't quite dead yet:

> And afterward the father of the youngster came to them, saying, "O brethren of ours! May I be your atonement. His [my] son is still writhing, so the knife has not yet been made unclean.[18]

This story makes sense only if ritual impurity is something different from moral impurity: murder in the temple pollutes the temple, not because it's violent, but because it produces a dead body. *Attempted* murder, which leaves the victim alive (at least long enough to get out of the temple), doesn't produce ritual impurity. This is exactly the point of the story: regardless of

14. Lev 7:21.
15. Deut 26:14.
16. Lev 22:3–6.
17. Num 5:16–26.
18. t. Yoma 1:12 (Neusner).

whether it was supposed to be a factual memory of something that actually happened, or whether it was an illustration like one of Jesus' parables, its purpose is to criticize the earlier temple authorities for misplaced priorities—for caring more about the ritual impurity of a corpse than about the moral impurity of violence.[19]

Another way to see the difference between ritual impurity and moral impurity is to explore what happens when the two are collapsed into a single system. As it turns out, this is pretty much what the Qumran sectarians did around the time of Jesus. As an isolated group living out in the desert, members of the community didn't have access to the temple; in fact, one of the reasons they lived away from Jerusalem was that they believed the temple had been corrupted by its current authorities. Therefore, ritual purity wouldn't affect members' access to the temple. But the community *did* make an effort to recreate holy or pure spaces among themselves, and this included how they prepared and ate food.[20] If we compare the community's "pure food" to the holy food eaten by the priests, then what's striking is that members were forbidden from eating this food, not just when they were *ritually* impure (as in the priestly regulations of the Old Testament), but also for *moral* infractions:

> If one is found among them who has lied knowingly concerning possessions, he shall be excluded from the pure food of the Many for a year and they shall withhold a quarter of his bread.... And if he has spoken angrily against one of the priests enrolled in the book, he will be punished for one year and shall be excluded, under sentence of death, from the pure food of the Many.... And whoever goes round defaming his fellow shall be excluded for one year from the pure food of the Many and shall be punished.... The person whose spirit turns aside from the foundation of the Community to betray the truth and walk in the stubbornness of his heart, if he comes back, shall be punished for two years; during the first year he shall not approach the pure food of the Many.[21]

Regulations like these are completely absent from Old Testament discussions of moral impurity. Sinful actions defile the sinner, the land, and the sanctuary—but they don't bar the sinner from going to the sanctuary or participating in sacrifices.

---

19. Klawans, *Impurity and Sin*, 121.
20. Newton, *Concept of Purity*, 21–26.
21. 1QS 6:24—7:19 (*DSSSE*).

Not All Dirt Is Sin

For Christians, the distinction between ritual impurity and moral impurity is especially important for understanding the ministry of Jesus. Some interpreters argue that Jesus radically opposed the purity regulations of his Jewish contemporaries, and even go so far as to claim that purity was the organizing principle behind a whole oppressive social system.[22] But this kind of analysis works only as long as we conflate ritual purity and moral purity.[23] Even in more nuanced discussions, it's all too easy to see purity issues where, in all likelihood, none existed. Breaking the Sabbath wouldn't have made Jesus and his disciples ritually impure;[24] Jesus certainly disagreed with the Pharisees about what actions are appropriate on the Sabbath, but the Torah never even hints that breaking the Sabbath makes a person ritually impure, and there's no reason to think that the Pharisees believed it did. Similarly, living with a man not her husband[25] wouldn't have made the woman at the well ritually impure.[26] (Nor is she, or the Syrophonecian woman, impure because they're Gentiles;[27] there's a rabbinic tradition that Gentiles are ritually impure in general, but the idea almost certainly developed later than the time of Jesus.[28])

Of course, the gospels clearly show Jesus opposing certain purity practices. For example, in the gospel of Mark, we see the Pharisees criticizing Jesus because his disciples eat without washing their hands.[29] Jesus responds with a general indictment of the Pharisees' priorities, arguing that they uphold human traditions while breaking God's actual commandments. Then he addresses impurity directly:

> "[T]here is nothing outside a person that by going in can defile, but the things that come out are what defile."
>
> When he had left the crowd and entered the house, his disciples asked him about the parable. He said to them, "Then do you also fail to understand? Do you not see that whatever goes into a person from outside cannot defile, since it enters, not the heart but the stomach, and goes out into the sewer?" (Thus he declared all

---

22. Borg, *Conflict*; Borg, *Contemporary Scholarship*, 107–12.
23. Malina, *New Testament World*; Neyrey, "Idea of Purity," 91–128.
24. Beck, *Unclean*, 173.
25. John 4:16–18.
26. Witherington, *Women*, 59–60.
27. Witherington, *Women*, 65.
28. Klawans, "Gentile Impurity," 285–312.
29. Mark 7:1–5.

foods clean.) And he said, "It is what comes out of a person that defiles. For it is from within, from the human heart, that evil intentions come: fornication, theft, murder, adultery, avarice, wickedness, deceit, licentiousness, envy, slander, pride, folly. All these evil things come from within, and they defile a person."[30]

Jesus unambiguously elevates moral purity over ritual purity—even to the point of stating that at least some physical ritual pollutants don't actually defile at all. (Mark's comment about clean and unclean foods—which we'll discuss in chapter 8—is most likely the result of Jesus' later followers reflecting on what his teachings mean for the dietary laws. It's clear that the disciples didn't understand Jesus' statement this way at the time; otherwise, it's hard to understand why whether to keep kosher was such an important issue in the early church.)

If this is the case, then does it really matter whether we're meticulous in describing exactly what kind of purity Jesus is talking about in each saying? At some point, isn't this just hair-splitting? I would argue that the answer is both yes and no. On the one hand, I think it's perfectly reasonable to adopt a purity framework as a lens for understanding Jesus' ministry and how he related to others. After all, Jesus did have serious things to say about purity systems. It's not even necessarily illegitimate to talk about purity in situations that the original people involved wouldn't have described with purity language; "uncleanness" is a powerful psychological metaphor for thinking about morality, and to some extent humans are going to do this whether we want to or not.[31]

But when we do this, there's real value in distinguishing between purity *as a useful modern tool for talking about social systems* and purity *as it was understood and experienced by the people we're talking about.* Otherwise, we're in danger of setting up a caricature of the Old Testament that distorts both the law itself and how Jesus interacted with it. As Amy-Jill Levine pithily puts it, we don't need to "make Judaism look bad in order to make Jesus look good."[32] Jesus already looks plenty good; he doesn't need our help.

For example, in the context of Mark 7, the specific practice that the Pharisees ask about isn't commanded by the written law in the Old Testament; some Jews, at some times, did extra hand-washing as an act

---

30. Mark 7:15–23.
31. Beck, *Unclean*, 33–50.
32. Levine, "Jewish Jesus."

of religious devotion.[33] So the issue at hand is already something beyond what's strictly commanded in the Torah. Moreover, Jesus rejects certain understandings of purity, but he doesn't reject the framework of purity altogether; he explicitly says that certain thoughts and actions *do* defile. And, in general, there's good reason to believe that Jesus by and large followed the regulations governing ritual purity.[34] So it's simply not accurate to say that Jesus opposed the purity system, full stop.

Becoming ritually impure is not a sin

In several respects, the ritual purity regulations of Leviticus and Numbers are far less stringent than many Christians think. As we've already discussed, the purification rituals aren't a punishment for becoming impure, because *becoming ritually impure is not a sin in the first place*.

This fact has long been appreciated by Jewish interpreters. The rabbis recognized an obligation for Jews to bury the dead, even though dead bodies are the most severe source of ritual impurity. The priests are forbidden to go near a corpse, except for close relatives,[35] and not even then for the high priest;[36] however, this prohibition for priests highlights the fact that ordinary people are *not* restricted in this way. It's fine—in fact, in later writings it's explicitly required—for non-priests to bury the dead, as long as they don't go to the sanctuary until they've completed the purification ritual. The apocryphal book of Tobit tells the story of a righteous man living in exile in Nineveh; among his many good deeds is his practice of burying dead Jews who have no other relatives to care for them, and Tobit is even willing to risk his life to do this.[37] The Mishnah rules that anyone who discovers a neglected body, *even a high priest*, must bury it.[38] Contrary to popular belief, the priest and the Levite in the parable of the good Samaritan wouldn't have been breaking the law by touching a corpse lying in the road.[39] On the contrary, if the priorities expressed in the Mishnah were already current in

---

33. Booth, *Laws of Purity*, 189–203.
34. Fredriksen, "Did Jesus Oppose?," 19–25, 42–48.
35. Lev 21:1–3.
36. Lev 21:10–11.
37. Tob 1:16–19; 2:3–8.
38. m. Naz. 7:1.
39. Luke 10:30–32; Borg, *Conflict*, 117–18; Derrett, *Law*, 211–17.

Jesus' time (possible, although we can't be certain), they would have been *obliged* to bury the man—and then purify themselves afterwards.

Similarly, the woman with the hemorrhage[40] wasn't "permanently cut . . . off from her husband and her religious community"[41] and wasn't prohibited from being in the crowd around Jesus.[42] At worst, she might have polluted the people she touched without their knowing it, but the odds are good that many or most of the people in the crowd were already impure anyway,[43] and were unlikely to go immediately from Galilee all the way to the temple without purifying themselves. (And it's not clear that *being touched by* the woman, as opposed to touching the woman oneself, would have been considered ritually defiling at all in the time of Jesus.[44]) In the same way, even though skin disease was a serious source of impurity that required the afflicted person to live separately, Jesus wasn't violating any Old Testament law by touching someone with the condition,[45] as long as he didn't go to the temple while he was impure.

In other words, Jesus did become ritually impure through contact with lepers, dead bodies,[46] and possibly the hemorrhaging woman, but *doing so wasn't a sin*, and most of his contemporaries wouldn't have thought it was. Ben Witherington argues that Jesus wouldn't have considered himself ritually impure after these encounters, on the basis of the Mark 7 passage where Jesus states that external things like foods don't defile[47] (and Witherington's own assumption that contact with ritual impurity was generally taboo). But I find this unconvincing; in that same passage, Jesus unambiguously says that sexual sins *do* defile, but he has no problem interacting with the woman caught in adultery[48] or the woman at the well,[49] and he even asks the latter for a drink. In other words, we don't need to appeal to a total rejection of purity in all its forms to explain why Jesus associates with both lepers and

---

40. Matt 9:20–21 // Mark 5:24–28 // Luke 8:42–44.
41. Evans, *Biblical Womanhood*, 169.
42. Hamerton-Kelly, *Poetics of Violence*, 94; Selvidge, "Mark 5:25–34," 619–23.
43. Sanders, *Judaism*, 375.
44. Fonrobert, *Menstrual Purity*, 193–95.
45. Beck, *Stranger God*, 74; Crossan, *Revolutionary Biography*, 83; Evans, *Biblical Womanhood*, 169–70.
46. Matt 9:23–25 // Mark 5:38–41 // Luke 8:52–54; Luke 7:12–14.
47. Witherington, *Women*, 74.
48. John 8:3–11.
49. John 4:7–18.

sinners. Jesus' words and actions are perfectly consistent with the difference we've been describing: moral impurity involves sin but doesn't pollute by contact; ritual impurity is the opposite. Jesus is clear that moral impurity is the more important of the two, but this was a less radical break from his contemporaries than many Christians realize.

And so we see that becoming ritually impure was an ordinary thing. Some Jews, mostly Pharisees, joined a voluntary association called the *chavurah* that was committed to following extra-stringent purity regulations;[50] however, the fact that they vowed (among other things) to "eat even ordinary food in purity"[51] shows that most people *didn't* worry about purity at every meal. Maimonides, writing much later, states this explicitly:

> Other persons that do not intend to enter the Sanctuary or touch any holy thing, are not guilty of any sin if they remain unclean as long as they like, and eat, according to their pleasure, ordinary food that has been in contact with unclean things.[52]

All this is not to say, of course, that ritual impurity can *never* be connected to sin. As we've already seen, neglecting the correct purification rituals is blameworthy, and so is going to the sanctuary—or eating holy food—while you're impure. There's also an ancient tradition among some rabbis connecting certain causes of impurity with sin. In particular, skin disease ("leprosy" in the older, less accurate translation) was sometimes thought to be a punishment, especially for slander:

> For ten reasons do plagues of leprosy come: idolatry, promiscuity, murder, profanation of God's name, blasphemy of God's name, robbing from the community, stealing what does not belong to a person, arrogance, gossiping, and grudging.[53]

After discussing the regulations for skin disease, Leviticus applies similar rules to mildew on cloth and walls in chapters 13 and 14. (Objects with this condition are quarantined and, if they don't improve, destroyed.) Maimonides suggests that diseases of walls, cloth, and skin could be progressive punishment for the unrepentant sinner:

> Now this change in garments and in houses . . . was a portent and a wonder among the Israelites to warn them against slanderous

---

50. Harrington, *Impurity Systems*, 274–81; Neusner, "Fellowship," 125–42.
51. t. Demai 2:2, translated in Neusner, "Fellowship," 130.
52. Maimonides, *Guide* 3.47.
53. *Lev. Rab.* 17.3 (Neusner).

speaking. For if a man uttered slander the walls of his house would suffer a change: if he repented the house would again become clean. But if he continued in his wickedness until the house was torn down, leather objects in his house on which he sat or lay would suffer a change: if he repented they would again become clean. But if he continued in his wickedness until they were burnt, his skin would suffer a change and he would become leprous and be set apart and exposed all alone until he should no more engage in the conversation of the wicked, which is raillery and slander.[54]

Another tradition creatively proposes that the quarantine procedures for an afflicted house could reveal hidden wrongdoing:

> A person says to his neighbor, "Lend me a qab of wheat," and the other says, "I don't have any." "A qab of barley...," "I don't have any." "A qab of dates," and he says to him, "I don't have any." A woman says to her friend, "Lend me a sieve," and she says, "I don't have any." "A sifter," and she says, "I don't have any." What does the Holy One, blessed be He, do? He brings leprosy signs into his house, and since the owner has to bring all of his utensils out into the street, everyone sees and says, "Didn't he say, 'I don't have any?' Now see how much wheat he has! How much barley he has! How many dates he has! A curse on the house of those who live therein!"[55]

Of course, this line of interpretation isn't universal in Judaism. Yet another tradition, for example, holds that God sent mildew into the Israelites' houses so that they would tear out holes in their walls and discover treasure hidden there by the Canaanites.[56] And even when skin disease is connected with punishment—something that happens occasionally but not systematically in the Old Testament itself[57]—the impurity isn't the punishment. The *disease* is the punishment, and impurity is just a natural consequence of the disease, punishment or not.

In discussions of another type of ritual impurity, that of a woman after childbirth, ancient rabbis pondered why the woman has to bring a sacrifice.[58] One possibility, of course, is that the woman is a sinner; Simeon ben Yoḥai was pretty sure he knew exactly what that sin was:

54. Maimonides, *Mishneh Torah*, Tsaraat 16:10.
55. *Lev. Rab.* 17.3 (Neusner).
56. *Lev. Rab.* 17.6.
57. Num 12:9–15; Deut 28:27; 2 Sam 3:29; 2 Kgs 5:26–27; 2 Chr 26:18–19.
58. Lev 12:6.

Not All Dirt Is Sin

> He replied: When she kneels in bearing she swears impetuously [because of the pain of childbirth] that she will have no intercourse with her husband. The Torah, therefore, ordained that she should bring a sacrifice [because she eventually violates her oath].[59]

Naturally, not all the rabbis bought this interpretation. But, conveniently, this idea also explains why the woman is impure after giving birth to a girl for twice as long as for a boy:[60]

> [On the birth of a] male with whom all rejoice she regrets her oath after seven days, [but on the birth of a female] about whom everybody is upset she regrets her oath after fourteen days.[61]

In my opinion—and that of plenty of other interpreters, both Jewish and Christian—the most faithful reading of this requirement is to understand that the woman hasn't sinned at all. (That doesn't explain the double impurity period for baby girls; I don't have a definitive answer for this, but we'll see some promising ideas in chapter 7.) All this is yet another reason to prefer "purification offering" as a translation of *chatta't*, rather than "sin offering." The purification rituals for a woman after childbirth,[62] a person cleansed of skin disease,[63] or a person cleansed of abnormal genital discharge[64] all involve a *chatta't*, even though nobody sinned. The *chatta't* can cleanse both moral impurity (the result of sin) and ritual impurity (the result of everyday physical defilements); the common ingredient is cleansing, not sin.

The consequences of ritual impurity

We've now seen the difference between ritual impurity and sin from two sides: sinning doesn't make someone ritually impure, and contracting ritual impurity isn't necessarily a sin. Now we turn to the next obvious question: if impurity isn't the same thing as sin, then what does it mean to be impure? After you encounter a dead body or start your period, what do you do?

---

59. b. Nid. 31b (Slotki).
60. Lev 12:2–5.
61. b. Nid. 31b (Slotki).
62. Lev 12:6.
63. Lev 14:1–12.
64. Lev 15:13–15, 25–30.

The misconception that ritual impurity is sinful is closely associated with mistaken ideas about what happens to people who are ritually impure. Many readers are influenced by the searing image of the person with skin disease, marked as different and separated from the community:

> The person who has the leprous disease shall wear torn clothes and let the hair of his head be disheveled; and he shall cover his upper lip and cry out, "Unclean, unclean." He shall remain unclean as long as he has the disease; he is unclean. He shall live alone; his dwelling shall be outside the camp.[65]

There's no denying that this is a severe isolation, and readers today will naturally be drawn—as they should be!—to questions about the relative value of the skin-diseased person's community membership compared to the community's values expressed through purity regulations.

But even in the Old Testament context, the isolation of the skin-diseased person *does not apply to everyone who's impure*. Numbers 5 describes ritually impure people leaving the camp while the Israelites were wandering in the wilderness,[66] but there's no evidence that this was the Israelites' regular practice in settled towns or cities. It's hard to imagine how such a thing would be remotely feasible; there would have been an enormous number of people outside the city walls at any given time: skin-diseased persons, anyone whose family member had died recently, any woman on her period, any man who had ejaculated in the last day or so, etc.

What about life *inside* the community? A. J. Jacobs[67] and Rachel Held Evans[68] experimented with following stringent purity regulations in contemporary daily life; both resolved to avoid communicating impurity by touch as far as possible. Jacobs, since he couldn't be sure who had ejaculated recently or was menstruating, decided not to touch anyone at all during his project—no handshakes or hugs. (Except his wife Julie, because he could know when she was on her period. She was still unhappy with his no-touch-during-her-period rule, and sat on all the chairs in their apartment to make them impure. I like her.) Evans focused on her own menstrual cycle and avoided all contact with her husband—one night in a tent outside, the rest in their spare bedroom.

---

65. Lev 13:45–46.
66. Num 5:1–4.
67. Jacobs, *Living Biblically*, 48–52.
68. Evans, *Biblical Womanhood*, 164–69.

Not All Dirt Is Sin

Both of these approaches depend, more or less, on the interpretation of the purity regulations that we discussed earlier: "if you do this, you will be unclean" means "don't do this; if you do, your punishment is that you will be unclean." But we've seen that this isn't how ritual impurity actually works in the Old Testament. A few situations are forbidden outright—men aren't allowed to have sex with a menstruating woman,[69] and the high priest isn't allowed to contact a dead body[70]—but, in general, the only legal consequence of being ritually impure is that you can't go to the sanctuary or touch holy things. And since some purification rituals involve special materials that aren't widely available, or are completed by a sacrifice at the temple, it's likely that lots of people—especially outside Jerusalem—were technically impure most of the time.[71]

Of course, this doesn't mean that ancient Israelites went around blithely ignoring ritual purity unless they happened to be going to the temple. For one thing, it's important to stay aware of your purity status so that you know when to purify, if necessary; nor is it the case that holy things were found only at the temple in Jerusalem. (A farmer, for example, would be very careful about purity when giving the local priest his share of the crop.) For another thing, there's always been diversity in Jewish practice, and it's clear that many Jews extended purity concerns far into daily life. In fact, many Jews in the Second Temple period aspired, basically, to be ritually pure as much as possible. But this didn't translate into avoiding ritual impurity at all costs; there may well have been some of that, but more notably, they developed a kind of quasi-impurity: after you become impure, washing won't make you officially ritually pure (because there are mandated waiting periods), but it can make you "pure enough" for important activities: eating, praying, or studying scripture.[72]

Besides the abundant literature from Qumran and the later rabbis that explicitly endorse this kind of purification, we see plenty of hints of the practice in the Apocrypha and the New Testament. Tobit, the man praised for burying his murdered countrymen in Nineveh, washes himself between burying a corpse and eating.[73] The full purification ritual takes seven days, but apparently bathing is a worthwhile first step. Judith, the legendary

69. Lev 18:19; 20:18.
70. Lev 21:10–11.
71. Maccoby, *Ritual and Morality*, 3–4.
72. Regev, "Pure Individualism," 177–81.
73. Tob 2:4–5.

heroine who tricks and beheads the captain of the Assyrian army, regularly bathes before praying.[74] Paul on his missionary journeys expects to find a place of prayer at the river.[75] The extra purification procedures adopted by members of the *chavurah*, and the hand-washing at issue in Mark 7 (which may in fact have been something promoted by the *chavurah*[76]), are examples of the same trend. Archaeological evidence from the Second Temple period tells the same story; there are ritual baths near cemeteries, and a surprisingly large number of stone vessels—which aren't susceptible to ritual impurity the way wood and pottery are—for drinking and storing liquids.[77] (It's no surprise that the jars Jesus uses to turn water into wine, which the text explains were meant for purification, are made of stone.[78])

So, on the one hand, in most cases the legal consequences of ritual impurity were pretty minimal; they only restricted you from the sanctuary and from holy food. On the other hand, plenty of Jews aspired to purity in their daily lives and went well beyond what was absolutely required. But even in their attempts to maintain ritual purity, we also see purity regulations being bent in ways that make them more inclusive, that allow more people to participate in community life. The Mishnah, for example, allows some of the purity laws to be relaxed at Passover[79] and other festivals.[80] This could partly be a practical necessity; if there are masses of people coming to Jerusalem, and you can't be certain that they're all scrupulous about ritual purity, a bit of "don't ask, don't tell" may be logistically helpful. But the Mishnah also allows celebration, in some cases, by people *known* to be ritually impure—a practice for which king Hezekiah's Passover gives scriptural precedent.[81] We see this same impulse toward including people in the much later *Shulchan Aruch*, a medieval Jewish legal code, which notes that some communities don't allow menstruating women in the synagogue (more on this below). It observes that these communities still let everybody come in on the important holy days, *explicitly* on the grounds that it's a real bummer if you miss Yom Kippur because you're on your period.

74. Jdt 12:5–8.
75. Acts 16:13.
76. Booth, *Laws of Purity*, 198–99.
77. Regev, "Pure Individualism," 181–86.
78. John 2:6.
79. m. Pesah. 7:4–7.
80. m. Hag. 3:6.
81. 2 Chr 30:17–20.

> And even in a place that follows the stringent practice, on the Days of Awe and other such occasions when many gather to enter the synagogue, [menstruants] are permitted to enter the synagogue like other women, because it will be great sadness for them if everyone gathers [in synagogue] but they stand outside.[82]

All the different approaches to ritual impurity that particular Jewish communities adopted, from the most lenient to the most strict, fall well within the range of impurity practices throughout the ancient world. The ancient Greeks, for example, considered many of the same things to be defiling—birth, sex, and death—and with similar consequences, primarily exclusion from the temple.[83] By contrast, pure and impure states in Zoroastrianism are part of the cosmic battle between good and evil. Therefore, it's vital for all believers to take the proper precautions, and perform the proper rituals or say the proper prayers, for an enormous variety of everyday activities: cutting hair or fingernails, urinating or defecating, having sex, bleeding, and more.[84]

Overall, what we see is that ritual impurity was more than a mechanism for excluding "undesirable" people from the community. Exclusion did happen in some cases, most notably the skin-diseased person, in ways that deserve our attention and prayerful thought. But it's also clear that Jews have always had a variety of responses to ritual impurity regulations, and plenty of those responses either show a sincere desire to draw closer to God or actually bend the rules in favor of including *more* people. This way of seeing the world also wasn't unique to ancient Israel; plenty of their neighbors did something similar, and so the purity system seems a lot like sacrifice in the sense that God was speaking the Israelites' language. All things considered, Christians—like Jesus—should oppose purity language and systems that are contrary to the full life that God intends for his people, but they should also—like Jesus—appreciate the ways that purity is a deeply human way of thinking about the world, and a way that we can honor the bodies God gave us and use them to draw closer to him.

---

82. *Shulchan Aruch*, quoted in Cohen, "Purity and Piety," 104.
83. Parker, *Miasma*, 53–54.
84. Choksy, *Purity and Pollution*, 80–110.

Menstruation and childbirth

I've just argued that the consequences of ritual impurity were generally a lot less severe than many modern readers assume. But there's one specific type of impurity that deserves a closer look in this context: impurity of women associated with the reproductive process. Leviticus is clear that menstruation[85] and childbirth[86] make a woman ritually impure. And there are Jewish communities today where women's daily life is seriously affected during their periods; Evans partly modeled her menstruation restrictions on modern Orthodox practice.[87] How can we say this wasn't a big deal?

First of all, the chapter in Leviticus that discusses menstruation doesn't only discuss menstruation. Leviticus 15 has a symmetrical structure that treats men and women in parallel:

A	Unusual male discharge (gonorrhea?)	Leviticus 15:2–15
B	Ordinary male discharge (ejaculation)	Leviticus 15:16–17
C	Intercourse between male and female (sex)	Leviticus 15:18
B	Ordinary female discharge (menstruation)	Leviticus 15:19–24
A	Unusual female discharge (non-menstrual bleeding)	Leviticus 15:25–30

The first half of the chapter discusses ritual impurity related to male genital discharges; the second half discusses ritual impurity related to female genital discharges. The beginning and end of the chapter deal with abnormal discharges; the sections just inside them deal with ordinary discharges; and the verse at the center deals with male-female intercourse. These regulations are remarkably even-handed; they don't single out women as especially impure. In fact, many ancient Jewish interpreters[88] (although not all[89]) deduced that sex pollutes, not because the woman is impure, but because the *man's semen* pollutes both of them. The verse itself refers to semen explicitly: "If a man lies with a woman *and has an emission of semen*, both of them shall bathe in water, and be unclean until the evening."[90] On this reading, when the priest Ahimelech offers to give David's companions

---

85. Lev 15:19–24.
86. Lev 12.
87. Evans, *Biblical Womanhood*, 152–55.
88. Gruber, "Purity and Impurity," 65–76.
89. Levine, *Leviticus*, 96; Maccoby, *Ritual and Morality*, 58–59.
90. Lev 15:18, emphasis added.

some holy bread, "provided that the young men have kept themselves from women,"⁹¹ Ahimelech isn't worried that women would have polluted the men; he's worried that the men would have polluted *themselves* by ejaculating during intercourse.

So, following this passage strictly, most men and women should expect to be ritually impure for a substantial portion of their adult lives. On the one hand, impurity from vaginal discharges seems to be a bit more severe than impurity from semen;⁹² on the other hand, it's not out of the question that a man could be impure for greater amounts of time, and on a less predictable schedule, than a woman.⁹³ A third-century Christian document, the *Didascalia Apostolorum*, tries to convince Christians not to bother about Jewish purity regulations for exactly this reason:

> For if, when a man shall have intercourse, or flux come out from him, he must be bathed, let him also wash his mattress—and he will have this travail and unceasing vexation: he will be bathing and he will be washing his clothes and his mattress, and he will not be able to do anything else.⁹⁴

And the laws of the Mishnah suggest that during the Second Temple period men really were concerned about this kind of ritual purity. Jews were expected to recite the Shema ("Hear, O Israel: The LORD is our God, the LORD alone"⁹⁵) twice a day—but not a man who was impure because of a genital discharge.

> One who has had a seminal discharge recites the Shema silently [literally "in his heart"]. And he may not recite either blessings before the Shema nor the blessings after it.⁹⁶

In fact, the rabbis put lots of restrictions on men after ejaculation that limited prayer and Torah study. (Remember that eating, prayer, and Torah were occasions whose purity devout Jews were especially eager to protect.) The intent of all this seems to have been to limit *male* sexuality—in the words of one Talmudic sage, "in order that scholars might not always be

---

91. 1 Sam 21:4.
92. Harrington, *Impurity Systems*, 220–29.
93. Kamionkowski, *Leviticus*, 151.
94. *Didascalia Apostolorum* 26.259.
95. Deut 6:4.
96. m. Ber. 3:4 (Neusner).

with their wives like [roosters]."[97] There was also special concern with discouraging sex during a woman's period, which is forbidden outright;[98] this is why many restrictions on husbands and wives attempted to avoid arousing the husband during this critical time.[99]

So the Old Testament laws themselves, and ancient understandings of them, didn't call for severe isolation of a woman on her period, and in fact didn't single out women for ritual impurity in general. But men who have recently ejaculated aren't generally treated as impure in contemporary Judaism, while ritual purification is practiced today in some Conservative and Orthodox households.[100] What happened?

The answer, at least in very general terms, is simple: most of the purity regulations eventually fell out of use, but some communities developed more stringent restrictions on menstruating women. It's possible (maybe; the evidence is sparse and hard to evaluate) that some upper-class women lived separately during their periods as early as the time of Jesus,[101] but otherwise the earliest evidence for severe restrictions comes from the sixth or seventh century; documents from that period don't literally send the woman out of the house, but they do forbid her from activities such as doing certain household chores, praying, or entering a synagogue or even a room of Hebrew books.[102] The practice seems to have started in Palestine and spread from there to other regions, and was vigorously debated throughout the Middle Ages. Maimonides thought the whole thing was ridiculous:

> [O]ther household chores, such as kneading, cooking, touching clothes, spreading out a mat—these acts are permitted even during the days of the menstrual period.... But if it is your custom to observe these additional safeguards, such as not to touch money and not to step on certain things and then proceed to cleanse herself by simply washing at sunset without immersing in a mikvah, such practice is absolute heresy, not grounded in any tradition and should be avoided.[103]

---

97. b. Ber. 22a (Simon).
98. Lev 18:19.
99. Cohen, "Menstruants and the Sacred," 279–80.
100. Meachem, "Abbreviated History," 33–36.
101. Harrington, *Impurity Systems*, 270–72.
102. Cohen, "Menstruants and the Sacred," 279–87.
103. Stitskin, "Responsum by Maimonides," 11.

(Although, to be fair, Maimonides was just as outraged by what he saw as these women's improper cleansing rituals as he was by unnecessary restrictions during their periods.[104])

But "what happened?" is a lot easier to answer than "*why* did it happen?" There are a lot of possible reasons, but none that completely explain why these particular changes happened when they did. The fact that the temple was destroyed may explain the decline of the purity system in general, but not why restrictions around menstruation got *more* strict. Conversely, after the temple was gone, Jews put more emphasis on everyday holiness in the home and synagogue; this could explain the increased attention to ritual purity around menstruation, but not why *only* menstruation was targeted. It's certainly possible that Jews were influenced by other cultures they came into contact with; in Zoroastrianism, for example, women *did* live separately while they were on their periods, and they could pollute certain things by touching or even looking at them.[105] But we know too little about the details of what this contact actually looked like to be certain that it really was a contributing factor. We could appeal to simple misogyny, but why would misogyny have kicked in at this particular time and place, and not earlier? Ultimately, we just don't know why ritual purity practices evolved in the particular way they did.

Before Christians start feeling too smug about all this, we should take a moment to point out that Christianity has done some very similar things, preventing menstruating women from entering churches or taking communion. Not only that, but the earliest Christian examples of this trend come centuries *before* the earliest clear Jewish examples.[106] As early as the third century, Dionysius of Alexandria reports approvingly that menstruating women stand in a front room, outside the church itself, to listen while others sing the psalms.[107] The *Didascalia Apostolorum*, written around the same time, reveals that some Christian women thought the Holy Spirit left them while they were on their periods.[108] Gregory the Great argues in the sixth century that menstruating women should be allowed to come to church and take communion, but he acknowledges that some women aren't comfortable doing so and concludes that's fine too:

104. Krakowski, "Maimonides' Menstrual Reform," 252–56.
105. Choksy, *Purity and Pollution*, 97–98.
106. Cohen, "Menstruants and the Sacred," 287–90.
107. Dionysius of Alexandria, *Letter to Basilides* (PG 10.1281–84).
108. *Didascalia Apostolorum* 26.256–59.

> Further, she ought not to be prohibited during these same days from receiving the mystery of holy communion. If, however, out of great reverence, she does not presume to receive, she is to be commended; but, if she should receive, she is not to be judged. For it is the part of good dispositions in some way to acknowledge their sins even where there is no sin.... And so females, when they consider themselves as being in their habit of sickness, if they presume not to approach the sacrament of the body and blood of the Lord, are to be commended for their right consideration. But when, out of the habit of a religious life, they are seized with a love of the same mystery, they are not to be restrained....[109]

(Interestingly, Gregory is much less lenient when it comes to men. His judgment is that a man with sex on his mind shouldn't be in church at all.)

> Further, a man after sleeping with his own wife ought not to enter the church unless washed with water, nor, even when washed, enter immediately.... [U]nless the fire of concupiscence in his mind should cool, he ought not to think himself worthy of the congregation of his brethren, seeing himself to be burdened with by lewdness of wrong desire.[110]

It's not just menstruation; Christian communities have also restricted mothers from coming back to church after they give birth. A ceremony that re-integrates new mothers (called "churching" in English-speaking areas) was practiced off and on for hundreds of years in the Catholic church, until as recently as the middle of the twentieth century. It usually wasn't required, but women often faced enormous social pressure to do it.

> Another belief firmly held by the older generations of women was that the mother didn't get strong until she was churched, nor that any food she cooked, or even served, would be fully nutritional until the churching was done, usually three weeks after the birth. It was a ceremony in the catholic church, a cleansing ceremony.... I don't know if it was obligatory but every woman was churched. If she weren't, the neighbours would not be pleased, as she might "bring a plague of rats about the place."
>
> It wasn't considered right for the mother to leave the house for any reason until she had been churched. I never knew for a long time what this ceremony meant. I thought that the mother was living in sin until this was done.... Any mother who didn't have

---

109. Gregory the Great, *NPNF*2, 78–79.
110. Gregory the Great, *NPNF*2, 79.

it done was considered to be almost pagan. The usual procedure was for the mother to kneel at the altar and hold a lighted candle while the priest prayed over her and blessed her with holy water. To me it was very similar to the christening of the baby when the devil was driven out.[111]

Some versions of the ceremony were explicitly supposed to purify the woman; others, especially in the nineteenth and twentieth centuries, were officially about thanksgiving or rejoicing. But since the priest spoke in Latin, the woman usually couldn't understand the words of the ritual at all, let alone analyze the nuances of exactly what psalms were recited or what prayers were said. The reality was that most women thought the ritual implied they were dirty and needed to be cleansed.[112]

What do we do with all this? On the one hand, the regulations about genital discharge in Leviticus 15 look awfully egalitarian, even if some later implementations of those rules were not. On the other hand, there's the unavoidable fact that these passages *have* been interpreted in ways that target women as especially impure. (Not to mention the fact that childbirth, a disproportionately female experience, is another source of ritual impurity—or the puzzling difference in impurity periods between male and female babies.) And, in general, it can be hard for modern readers to understand the value of any of these ritual impurity laws. Fine, they're not about sin; but what positive value could they possibly have?

We'll discuss what meaning ritual impurity might have in chapter 7. For now, we'll end with the observation that some contemporary women continue to observe purity regulations around their periods, and some find it meaningful, beautiful, or even empowering. This isn't a universal experience, of course; there are also plenty of women who find the rules burdensome or embarrassing. But it's been observed that the complicated rabbinic regulations around menstrual impurity do, in one way, show a high regard for women: they trust women to understand and follow highly complex rules for how to identify the start of a period. What if you find blood on your clothes? Is it below the belt? What if you find it on your inner thigh? Outer thigh? What if you squished a louse that day; could the blood be from the louse? There's no indication that a priest, or even the woman's husband, is supposed to double-check to make sure she's doing everything

---

111. Irish women, quoted in O'Connor, "Listening to Tradition," 84–85.
112. Roll, "Old Rite," 117–41.

right.[113] Not that menstruation is a paradise of female self-determination; the Talmud makes it very clear that (male) rabbis are the final authorities.[114] But there's also evidence that some women have used these regulations to carve out a bit of autonomy:

> Samuel . . . wanted to have sexual relations with his wife. She said to him, "I am unclean." On the next day, she said to him, "I am clean." He said to her, "Yesterday you told me you were unclean, and today you tell me you are clean!" She said to him, "At that time I didn't really have the strength for it." He came and asked Rab. He said to him, "Since she brought a reasonable explanation for her original statement, she is believed."[115]

To be clear, I'm not personally in favor of introducing these purity rituals in communities that don't currently have them. It's all too easy for regulations like these, even with the best of intentions, to be used to teach some people that they're worth less than others. But I also want to listen to, and learn from, those who experience these practices as meaningful and life-giving. If modern readers want to discover a way to read Leviticus that doesn't seem oppressive and alienating, women who have actually lived with the practice would be a good place to start.

> This mitzvah fits with my feminist belief that as women we should know our own bodies and cycles and that the relationship should be going along with the rhythm of a woman's natural cycles. The laws respect that. The fact that you have periods in your relationship without contact, what that allows is for the person to really remain an individual. . . . It allows you to maintain your own space, your own individuality, and you don't have someone who has sort of a claim to your body all the time—your body is your own for half the month. I think that all those things are really good.[116]

---

113. Wegner, *Chattel or Person?*, 162–65.
114. Fonrobert, *Menstrual Purity*, 40–127.
115. y. Ketub. 2:5 (Neusner).
116. Orthodox woman, quoted in Marmon, "Reflections," 236.

7

THE PURPOSE OF RITUAL PURITY

I SHOULD APOLOGIZE RIGHT off the bat for the title of this chapter. It makes a promise that the chapter can't deliver on; we're not going to arrive at a tidy explanation of ritual purity that ties everything up with a neat bow. In fact, in my opinion, ritual purity is a lot like sacrifice: many interpretations have been proposed in both Jewish and Christian traditions, and we don't necessarily have to choose just one.

If the last chapter was essentially deconstructive—arguing that ritual purity does *not* work like many Christians think—then this chapter tries to be constructive. If ritual purity were about sin, then it would be pretty obvious why Leviticus regulates it; after all, sin is an important topic in the Old Testament generally. But since we've established that ritual purity is *not* about sin, what other purpose could it serve? And, most relevant for Christians who don't follow ritual purity regulations today, is there any point in continuing to read the parts of scripture that talk about it?

Ritual purity is not about hygiene

Before we move on to the real constructive work, we have one last bit of deconstruction to do. One of the most popular modern understandings of ritual purity is that, at least in part, it's a kind of primitive hygiene.[1] Depending on your perspective, either it shows that the ancient Israelites

---

1. Albright, *Yahweh*, 180–81; Gafney, *Womanist Midrash*, 107–8; Kalas, *Gospel*, 130–32; Levine, *Leviticus*, 249–50.

had some kind of latent but advanced germ theory, or it's evidence that God enacted the regulations in order to ensure a basic level of sanitation.

It's easy to see why this theory is attractive today. On the surface, the ritual purity rules look a lot like basic hygiene: special treatment of bodily fluids, mandated washings, quarantine procedures. Also, preventing sickness is an appealing rationale for such detailed rules; surely anyone could get behind *that* goal. Judaism isn't the only tradition that attracts this kind of reasoning; purity practices in Hinduism,[2] Buddhism,[3] Islam,[4] Zoroastrianism,[5] and many other traditions[6] have all been connected to physical health by modern commentators.

Here's the problem: the regulations surrounding ritual impurity in the Old Testament aren't actually very good hygiene rules. For example, the *only* bodily fluids that are regulated are genital discharges.[7] Plenty of other bodily fluids are also carriers of infection, if not worse: snot, pus, vomit, blood, urine, feces, etc. Unless they're coming out of your penis or your vagina, Leviticus has nothing to say about them. (There's a regulation that a man with an irregular genital discharge makes people unclean if he spits on them,[8] but the problem isn't the spit itself; it's the fact that the spitter has a discharge from his penis. Again, we're back to the uniqueness of genital discharges. There's also a rule that requires soldiers to defecate in a hole in the ground outside the military camp[9]—but why only in a military context? And why no rule that he has to wash his hands afterwards? At any rate, even at the military camp, feces don't cause ritual impurity.)

It's not as though these other bodily fluids would have been too hard to regulate. You could imagine very simple public sanitation rules that would have been no more complicated than what we actually see in Leviticus:

> If a man sneezes, he shall cover his face with his elbow. If he sneezes onto his hand, he shall be unclean. He must wash his hands with water; then he will be clean.

2. Amin, "Hinduism," 58–62.
3. Dhirasekera, "Observations," 63–65.
4. El Bedri, "Health Education," 79–88.
5. Modi, *Religious Ceremonies*, 103–4, 157–60.
6. Douglas, *Purity and Danger*, 29–32.
7. Lev 15.
8. Lev 15:8.
9. Deut 23:12–13.

The Purpose of Ritual Purity

> If a man vomits, he shall be unclean. Any object upon which the vomit falls shall be unclean; it must be washed with water. Any person the vomit touches must bathe himself and wash his clothes; he will be unclean until evening. The man who vomits shall be unclean until one full day has passed in which he does not vomit; then he will be clean. [This last part is a rule used by many day care centers and elementary schools.]
>
> If a man burns with fever, or if he coughs, or if he becomes unable to smell, he is unclean. All the days of his uncleanness he shall not approach nearer than four cubits to another person. He shall cover his nose and mouth with a garment and live apart from his fellows. After he no longer burns with fever, and does not cough, he shall wait fourteen days; he must bathe himself and wash his clothes, and then he will be clean.

Similarly, infectious diseases in general aren't regulated; only skin diseases (and conditions that cause genital discharges) are targeted. Contrary to what some interpreters have assumed,[10] touching Peter's sick mother-in-law would *not* have made Jesus ritually impure. Dead bodies are the most severe source of ritual impurity, but it doesn't matter whether the person died of an infectious disease or a heart attack; moreover, even a human bone or a grave has the same effect,[11] even though at some point these things stop being contagious.

Other purity regulations show a remarkable disregard for the way infection actually works. If a house is suspected of mildew, the people who live there are explicitly instructed to get everything out of the house *before* the priest shows up to inspect it, because anything still in the house when the priest makes an official pronouncement will be unclean.[12] If we were really talking about dangerous biological contaminants, it shouldn't matter when the priest declares something unclean. Just because a doctor hasn't diagnosed you yet with the flu doesn't mean you can't infect me now.

It's possible, of course, that the ancient Israelites were *trying* to implement basic sanitation, and they just weren't very good at it. Or it's possible that God didn't give them more medically precise rules because they wouldn't have been able to follow them—although I find that argument pretty strained. A better approach to all this is to give up our modern sense

---

10. Witherington, *Women*, 67–68.
11. Num 19:16.
12. Lev 14:36.

of what the purity regulations *ought* to be about, and accept that ritual purity was never supposed to be about hygiene in the first place. Instead of trying to force these practices into a sanitation mold, we can learn more by listening to them on their own terms.

Matter out of place

The anthropologist Mary Douglas had a profound effect on modern understandings of Leviticus with her book *Purity and Danger*. Where an earlier generation of scholars dismissed purity rules as primitive or magical thinking—or else reduced them to sanitation codes—Douglas approached them holistically and asked what meaning they might have within the larger systems in which they were embedded. Douglas argued that it's a fallacy to distinguish between superstitious purity beliefs and modern, logical, scientific hygiene practices; everyone, she says, relies on symbolism and categories in order to think about dirt.

> [Dirt] is a relative idea. Shoes are not dirty in themselves, but it is dirty to place them on the dining-table; food is not dirty in itself, but it is dirty to leave cooking utensils in the bedroom, or food bespattered on clothing; similarly, bathroom equipment in the drawing room; clothing lying on chairs; out-door things in-doors; upstairs things downstairs; under-clothing appearing where over-clothing should be, and so on. In short, our pollution behavior is the reaction which condemns any object or idea likely to confuse or contradict cherished classifications.[13]

Adopting a phrase of William James's, Douglas summarizes dirt as "matter out of place." This way of thinking about purity has two major implications. First, it gives us very little leeway to be smug about how our ideas of cleanliness are so much more advanced than other cultures'. True, scientists have learned a great deal about infectious disease, and sanitation has made enormous progress in the last few centuries; I'm grateful to have been born in the late twentieth century. But our everyday behavior is influenced just as much by culture as it is by science. When I wash my hands after a trip to the bathroom, it's not because I've been reading up on the latest public health research; it's because my culture has taught me that not doing so is gross. In this case my culture happens to be right; washing your hands really does make it less likely that you'll get sick (or get others sick).

13. Douglas, *Purity and Danger*, 35–36.

The Purpose of Ritual Purity

But there are plenty of other cases where we're conditioned to think about impurity in ways that aren't perfectly logical. I *know* that if I drop an apple slice on the ground and a little dirt gets on it, the slice is still fine to eat—but I just can't do it. And I know it isn't strictly necessary to shower every day, but I still feel icky if I don't.

The second major implication of Douglas's approach is that it makes sense to look for meaning in purity systems. If dirt is matter out of place, then dirt can't exist without a system—without ideas about where things *should* be. If impurity is something that has transgressed boundaries, then by definition the existence of impurity entails the existence of boundaries, and the classification scheme that defines them.

Douglas mostly focuses on how to understand dietary laws, clean and unclean animals, along these lines; we'll discuss this in more detail in chapter 8. But impurity as boundary-crossing can also be related to ritual impurity. Genital discharges, for example, are a very literal example of substances leaving the human body, crossing the boundary that separates the body from the rest of the world, violating its wholeness and completeness.[14] Similarly, this idea could explain why disease in general isn't targeted for purity regulations; only skin diseases, which specifically affect the boundaries of a person's body. This line of thinking gets at something deeply real about human psychology; many of our judgments about what's unclean or disgusting involve things that cross the boundaries of the body.[15]

Douglas's ideas are an important corrective to some unhelpful ways of talking about ritual purity. But they don't fully explain everything we might want to understand about how purity works, either in Leviticus or in human societies more generally. For one thing, as Douglas herself acknowledges,[16] not everything that's "out of place" is actually classified as impure. A car that's parked in a handicap spot without the appropriate tag isn't dirty; it's just rude. (Some of the excessively enthusiastic attempts to apply ritual impurity to all sorts of aspects of Jewish life in the time of Jesus that we saw in chapter 6 were inspired in part by Douglas's work.[17]) And, on the other hand, some things are dirty regardless of where you put them. I have strong opinions about the proper place of vomit—in the toilet is much

---

14. Douglas, *Purity and Danger*, 51–52.
15. Beck, *Unclean*, 15–16.
16. Douglas, *Purity and Danger*, 52.
17. Borg, *Conflict*, 9; Malina, *New Testament World*, 126; Neyrey, "Idea of Purity," 91–128.

better than in a bed—but even after it's been flushed into the sewer, the vomit itself is still disgusting.

Moreover, the relationship between dirt and culture doesn't flow in only one direction. The fact that our society considers it dirty to not wash your hands isn't a happy coincidence; we believe this because medical professionals like Ignaz Semmelweis, Florence Nightingale, and Joseph Lister worked hard to convince people that hand-washing really does keep us healthy. In other words, the dirt can come first: once we conclude that unwashed hands are hygienically dangerous, we decide that it's improper not to wash them. It's not just categories that create dirt; dirt can drive categories, too.

To come back to an analogy from chapter 3, in my opinion the best way to think about purity-as-disorder is to treat it as one clove in a bulb of garlic. The more closely we look at how ideas about purity interact with other social forms of classification, the more disorder looks like one element of a complex interconnected system: it's closely linked to how we create and enforce categories, to psychological feelings of disgust, and to ideas about health and wholeness; but no single part of the network drives all the others.

The best legacy of Douglas's work is the way it encouraged interpreters to see purity regulations as part of a coherent system, rather than treating them as a collection of unrelated and arbitrary rules. We may not agree with her on the details of what that system is, but we can certainly agree that it's not wrong to look for theology even in Leviticus.

Life and death

So far we've established that the regulations surrounding ritual impurity are likely to be meaningful, that this meaning goes beyond simple hygiene, and that it's also probably more than just disorder. It seems worthwhile to explore whether the major sources of ritual impurity—dead bodies, skin diseases, and genital emissions—have anything in common, something that might help us understand why these particular conditions cause impurity and not others. Of course, there's no guarantee that all types of impurity can be reduced to a single principle. Just as we saw that the different types of sacrifices, although they all express the relationship between humans and God, deal with different aspects of that relationship, we may very well find that ritual impurity may express multiple distinct understandings of the human condition.

As it turns out, though, commentators regularly point out that there *does* seem to be a common thread running through the sources of ritual impurity: the boundary between life and death. A corpse, of course, is obviously connected with death. Skin disease is somewhat less obvious; disease, of course, can lead to death, but the kinds of conditions described in Leviticus 13 aren't likely to be that dangerous, and plenty of other diseases are far worse. But there's reason to think that skin diseases in particular were culturally connected with the *appearance* of death. When God punishes Miriam with a skin disease for rebelling against Moses, Aaron makes this connection explicitly:

> When the cloud went away from over the tent, Miriam had become leprous, as white as snow. And Aaron turned towards Miriam and saw that she was leprous. Then Aaron said to Moses, "Oh, my lord, do not punish us for a sin that we have so foolishly committed. Do not let her be like one stillborn, whose flesh is half consumed when it comes out of its mother's womb."[18]

So it seems that skin diseases are ritually impure, not because those who have them are literally at death's door, but because they represent the *appearance* of death. As for mildew in clothes and walls, the structure of Leviticus 13–14 makes it very clear that these conditions cause ritual impurity on analogy with skin diseases. The regulations surrounding mildew are interwoven with the regulations for skin diseases, and the procedures and even a lot of the vocabulary are the same.

So far, the things that cause ritual impurity seem to be closely associated with death, full stop. But genital discharges, especially ordinary ones, aren't deadly at all. Rather, sexual intercourse—and, by extension, the organs associated with it—is the means by which new *life* is brought into the world. This is one reason to suspect that it's the boundary between life and death, rather than simply death itself, that triggers ritual impurity. Neither the beginning nor the end of life is to be taken lightly.

Moreover, if ritual impurity is related to the boundary between life and death, rather than death alone, then we come back to a Douglas-like understanding after all. In fact, as we'll see in chapter 8, respecting boundaries—maintaining distinctions—is deeply embedded in the story of creation itself, and that story is reflected all over the place in sanctuary

---

18. Num 12:10–12.

worship. Death may not be part of God's original design, but it, like the rest of good-but-fallen creation, is subject to his ordering and his authority. Life flourishes when we respect limits, when we don't try to encroach on what isn't rightfully ours.

So there's good reason to see connections between ritual impurity and both life and death. (This idea also gives us one plausible explanation for the fact that a woman is impure twice as long after giving birth to a girl as after giving birth to a boy: a girl, as a potential future child-bearer herself, represents even *more* life.) But it's also fair to acknowledge that the system seems just a tad weighted towards the death side of the scale. It would be hard to interpret corpse-impurity as somehow actually being about life, whereas it's not too much of a stretch to see the loss of these important genital fluids as, symbolically, a kind of loss of life. And folk beliefs that menstrual blood in particular is *literally* deadly were common, although not universal, across the ancient world. Pliny the Elder, a first-century Roman writer, famously lists the terrible things that women on their periods can do:

> [I]f this female power should issue when the moon or sun is in eclipse, it will cause irremediable harm; no less harm if there is no moon; at such seasons sexual intercourse brings disease and death upon the man; purple too is tarnished then by the woman's touch. So much greater then is the power of a menstruous woman. But at any other time of menstruation, if women go round the cornfield naked, caterpillars, worms, beetles and other vermin fall to the ground.... Care must be taken that they do not do so at sunrise, for the crop dries up, they say, the young vines are irremediably harmed by the touch, and rue and ivy, plants of the highest medicinal power, die at once. I have said much about this virulent discharge, but besides it is certain that when their hives are touched by women in this state bees fly away, at their touch linen they are boiling turns black, the edge of razors is blunted, brass contracts copper rust and a foul smell, especially if the moon is waning at the time, mares in foal if touched miscarry.... miscarriage is caused by a smear, or even if a woman with child steps over it.[19]

Childbirth, too, has historically been a dangerous time for both mother and baby; even an uneventful birth, where nothing goes wrong, is a "brush with death."[20]

---

19. Pliny, *Nat.* 28.23.
20. Morrow, *Biblical Law*, 140; Riskin, *Vayikra*, 115.

The Purpose of Ritual Purity

Overall, although a connection between ritual impurity and death is one that a lot of interpreters find convincing,[21] not everyone buys the claim that genital emissions fit neatly into this system. Also, ordinary bleeding seems far more associated with death than menstrual bleeding; people literally bleed to death in a way that menstruating women usually don't. And yet, despite claims to the contrary,[22] non-menstrual blood isn't ritually impure.[23] At some point, we run the risk of circular reasoning: How do we know ritual impurity represents death? Because genital discharges represent death. How do we know genital discharges represent death? Because they're ritually impure.

Yet another view is that ritual impurity isn't about only one thing (life/death, or just death); it's about two things (death and sex).[24] We can relate these two things back to one thing by observing that both are things God doesn't do (God doesn't die and doesn't have sexual intercourse), or we can observe that death and sex are psychologically linked[25]—but eventually we come to a place where I'm not fully convinced of the value of calculating the precise number of First Principles of Ritual Impurity. The garlic cloves are tightly packed indeed.

At any rate, even if it doesn't answer every question we have about ritual impurity, the connection to life and death certainly helps with at least some of them. For one thing, general human ideas about uncleanness are closely connected to our ideas about death[26] (and sex![27]). Once again, ritual purity is getting at something fundamental about human psychology. It's probably not a coincidence that similar conditions pop up repeatedly in the ritual purity systems of other cultures. Birth, sex, and death (among other things) were all involved in the pollution systems of ancient Greece.[28] Zoroastrian theology explicitly connects purity with life and death; death and decay are weapons of the forces of evil, and therefore part of humans'

---

21. Eilberg-Schwartz, *Savage*, 183–85; Kiuchi, *Leviticus*, 38–39; Milgrom, *Leviticus 1–16*, 766–68, 1002–4; Morales, *Who Shall Ascend?*, 157–59; Riskin, *Vayikra*, 113–15; Sacks, *Leviticus*, 183–84; Wenham, *Leviticus*, 188; Willis, *Leviticus*, 103–4.

22. Choksy, *Purity and Pollution*, 103; Milgrom, *Leviticus 1–16*, 767.

23. Maccoby, *Ritual and Morality*, 31.

24. Frymer-Kensky, "Pollution," 400–401; Klawans, *Symbolism and Supersessionism*, 56–58.

25. Beck, *Unclean*, 157–59.

26. Beck, *Unclean*, 146–53.

27. Beck, *Unclean*, 157–64.

28. Parker, *Miasma*.

fight against evil is maintaining ritual purity. This includes separating themselves and all pure organisms and substances from death and anything that represents death.[29]

We're also ready now to come back to the purifying power of blood. In chapter 4, we observed that sacrificial rituals use blood to cleanse the pollution of sin, and that the closest we have to an explanation for this is a statement that "life is in the blood:"

> If anyone of the house of Israel or of the aliens who reside among them eats any blood, I will set my face against that person who eats blood, and will cut that person off from the people. For *the life of the flesh is in the blood*; and I have given it to you for making atonement for your lives on the altar; for, as life, it is the blood that makes atonement.[30]

A creature's blood represents its life; that much makes sense. It's also clear that humans don't take this blood on their own initiative; the blood, and its life, are a sacred gift from the God who is lord of both. And now, having seen the connections between ritual impurity and the boundary between life and death, more pieces start to fall into place. Sacrifices cleanse ritual impurity too, not just moral impurity; the rituals for purification after childbirth,[31] skin disease,[32] and abnormal discharge[33] involve sacrifices of various kinds (*chatta't, 'olah*, and even *'asham*, depending on the type of ritual impurity). What better substance to purify pollution coming from the forces of death than something that represents life itself?

Of course, chapter 6 made a big deal about how ritual impurity is *not* the same thing as moral impurity. But, with that distinction clearly established, we can still recognize connections between the two. In fact, we have more than just the indirect connections we've established so far (sin is like dirt; some other dirt is like death; therefore, maybe sin is like death)—the Old Testament directly equates living in God's ways with life and leaving those ways with death, from the danger of death associated with the tree of knowledge of good and evil in the garden of Eden[34] to affirmations that God's law is good and life-giving:

29. Choksy, *Purity and Pollution*, 2–19.
30. Lev 17:10–11, emphasis added.
31. Lev 12:6.
32. Lev 14:10–20.
33. Lev 15:13–15, 28–30.
34. Gen 2:16–17.

The Purpose of Ritual Purity

> You shall keep my statutes and my ordinances; *by doing so one shall live*: I am the Lord.[35]

> I call heaven and earth to witness against you today that I have set before you life and death, blessings and curses. *Choose life* so that you and your descendants may live, loving the Lord your God, obeying him, and holding fast to him; *for that means life to you* and length of days, so that you may live in the land that the Lord swore to give to your ancestors, to Abraham, to Isaac, and to Jacob.[36]

Christians, of course, continue to affirm the same thing: that "the wages of sin is death."[37] The blood of Jesus, representing his life poured out for others, overwhelms the powers of sin and death and brings life to the world.

Again, we can make all these connections without having to choose one system or idea as primary, as the Thing That Explains All the Other Things. Some scholars have proposed that either ritual or moral impurity is the basic system, and that the other is just a symbolic representation of the first. One interpretation, for example, is that ritual impurity from skin disease and childbirth serves to remind humans of their inherent sinfulness[38] and encourage moral purity.[39] (But there's no universal agreement on *which* system is fundamental.[40] At least one proposal tries to make *both* systems symbols of the other, which as Klawans wryly notes would have to mean that "ritual defilement serves to symbolize its own metaphorization."[41]) Trying to force one system into the framework of the other is ultimately never satisfying; there are always leftover pieces that don't quite fit. All this is unnecessary if we accept that the Old Testament world, like ours, consists of a bunch of interlocking systems that mutually reinforce each other: ritual impurity, moral impurity, sacrifice, sin, death, life, and so on. They look more like a network than a pyramid: garlic, not onions.

---

35. Lev 18:5, emphasis added.
36. Deut 30:19–20, emphasis added.
37. Rom 6:23.
38. Kiuchi, *Leviticus*, 39–40, 220, 241–42, 286–88; Morales, *Who Shall Ascend?*, 159–62; Wenham, *Leviticus*, 59.
39. Sklar, *Leviticus*, 49.
40. Klawans, *Impurity and Sin*, 37–38.
41. Klawans, *Impurity and Sin*, 37.

Reverence

We have one more aspect of ritual impurity to consider. Maimonides gives a justification for purity regulations that's different from anything we've seen so far:

> But when we continually see an object, however sublime it may be, our regard for that object will be lessened, and the impression we have received of it will be weakened. Our Sages, considering this fact, said that we should not enter the Temple whenever we liked.... For this reason the unclean were not allowed to enter the sanctuary, although there are so many kinds of uncleanliness, that [at the same time] only a few people are clean.[42]

Incidentally, this description is yet another piece of evidence that, under the Old Testament law, most people were ritually impure most of the time. But what we're interested in here is the way Maimonides suggests that ritual impurity is intended to cultivate respect for the sanctuary, by limiting who can go there and when. In other words, ritual impurity uses separation to encourage reverence, a kind of "absence makes the heart grow fonder." A related idea is that ritual purity is like palace etiquette, special rules that apply in the presence of a ruler.[43]

Maimonides's idea is already pretty different from what a lot of modern readers associate with ritual impurity. But there's a twist on this approach that may seem even more radical: what if *ritually impure things themselves* have that condition as a sign of the reverence they deserve? That is, what if ritual impurity formalizes, not just our reactions of disgust, but also our reactions of awe?

Let's start with some specific examples. The most severe source of ritual impurity is a human corpse; the affected person is impure for seven days, and needs two ritual sprinklings in order to be purified, plus a bath and laundering.[44] Corpse impurity is extremely contagious: you don't have to physically touch the dead body; even being in the same tent is enough (contamination by overhang).[45] By contrast, the dead body of an animal is

---

42. Maimonides, *Guide* 3.47.
43. Maccoby, *Ritual and Morality*, 9–11, 206.
44. Num 19:18–19.
45. Num 19:14–15.

far less potent: at worst, it causes a one-day ritual impurity, and it contaminates only by touch.[46]

Do these differences mean that the Old Testament values people less than animals? Hardly! Suppose I visit your home and we're sitting in the living room. If you tell me, "My mother died in this room," I'm going to experience something like awe or reverence; we're in a special place (not for a happy reason, but important nevertheless). But if you tell me, "My goldfish died in this room"—well, I'm probably not going to have that feeling quite as strongly. (And with this example I don't mean to devalue the feelings of anyone who *is* seriously upset by the death of a fish. If you tell me about your goldfish and it's clear that you're feeling some kind of awe in the room, that just makes the same point in a different way—I would interpret your seriousness as an indication that you have *more* respect for the fish, not less.)

The idea that ritual impurity can be a sign of respect shows up explicitly in the Mishnah. One passage records a disagreement between Sadducees and Pharisees, where the Sadducees are flabbergasted by the Pharisees' ruling that touching scripture makes a person's hands unclean. The Pharisees argue that books, like dead bodies, are more contagious the more highly they're valued:

> Say Sadducees: "We complain against you, Pharisees. For you say, 'Holy Scriptures impart uncleanness to hands, but the books of Homer do not impart uncleanness to hands.'" Said Rabban Yohanan b. Zakkai, "And do we have against the Pharisees only this matter alone? Lo, they say, 'The bones of an ass are clean, but the bones of Yohanan, high priest, are unclean.'" They said to him, "According to their preciousness is their uncleanness. So that a man should not make the bones of his father and mother into spoons." He said to them, "So too Holy Scriptures: According to their preciousness is their uncleanness. But the books of Homer, which are not precious, do not impart uncleanness to hands."[47]

Similarly, the Mishnah rules that menstrual blood from a Gentile woman doesn't pollute,[48] and in fact Gentiles in general aren't susceptible to impurity.[49] This is definitely not a sign of high esteem for Gentiles!

---

46. Lev 11:24–40.
47. m. Yad. 4:6 (Neusner).
48. m. Nid. 7:3.
49. Maccoby, *Ritual and Morality*, 8–11.

Misreading Ritual

We see similar phenomena in other impurity systems. In ancient Greece, human corpses were considered so polluting that they had to be buried outside the town. But many communities buried children within the boundaries; most likely, this reflects children's low status, not high status. Similarly, it's possible (although we have very little evidence either way) that an enslaved person's body would have been considered less defiling than a free person's.[50] In Zoroastrianism, the body of a righteous man is much more impure than the body of an evil man or of a non-Zoroastrian, because it must have taken a lot more demons to fight against the righteous man's good deeds and kill him.[51]

These examples make the *social* dimensions of impurity (as opposed to the hygienic dimensions) especially clear. Robert Parker compares corpse-impurity in ancient Greece to going into mourning: a death could pollute relatives even when they were many miles away, close relatives stayed polluted for longer than mere acquaintances, and even commemorating the anniversary of a death could be mildly polluting.[52] Clearly, we're not dealing with germs; these rules map suspiciously well onto social expectations about grief after the death of a friend or relative.

It's important not to take this perspective on ritual impurity too far. It would *not* be accurate to say that we have impurity all backwards, and that impurity actually equals respect; Leviticus doesn't demonstrate a secret admiration for skin diseases or gonorrhea. In a sense, we're encountering the phenomenon, not universal but surprisingly common, in which the categories of "holy" and "polluted"—usually polar opposites—occasionally converge.[53] The important nuance here is that the categories don't *always* converge; that is, holiness and pollution are *not* the same thing. In ancient Greece, not only children but also occasionally local heroes could be buried inside the town walls, but not for the same reasons: whereas children were apparently not valued enough to cause pollution, admirers of a VIP could get a waiver to build him a fancy public tomb and hold special commemorative ceremonies.[54]

So we should be cautious before we draw simple conclusions about what the ancient Israelites did or didn't value. But I also believe that,

50. Parker, *Miasma*, 41.
51. Choksy, *Purity and Pollution*, 16–17.
52. Parker, *Miasma*, 38–40.
53. Douglas, *Purity and Danger*, 7–11.
54. Parker, *Miasma*, 41–43.

carefully handled, impurity-as-reverence can be a valuable tool for modern readers who want to appreciate these passages as scripture. Not as apologetics ("oh, ancient Israelite society wasn't actually sexist"—no, it definitely was), nor as a manual for contemporary life ("let's start shunning people with psoriasis; they'll feel so respected!"), but as a way for scripture to teach us to see the image of God in places where we aren't used to looking for it.

For example, what happens if we learn from the genital discharge regulations of Leviticus 15 that *all* bodies, not just healthy male ones, are created by God and worthy of respect? Some contemporary Orthodox women interpret rituals around menstruation in precisely this way;[55] even those of us who don't follow these practices can still adopt a similar reading. I tend to doubt that ancient Jewish women experienced the double time of impurity following the birth of a girl as a sign of respect for their daughters, but that doesn't mean *we* can't read it that way now. These practices create space around embodied experiences, in ways that we could read as protective (people who are ritually impure are relieved of certain duties and allowed time to recharge) or as deferential (they stand at the boundary between life and death, which we should not approach thoughtlessly). Either way, Leviticus doesn't speak about genital discharges or the mess of childbirth in embarrassed whispers; it uses the full range of embodied living to invite us to pause and consider the presence of God among us.

Similarly, the regulations about skin diseases required priests (and possibly women in priestly families![56]) to give careful attention to something many of us would consider a disfigurement. What if we read these rules as an invitation to God's people, as a "holy priesthood,"[57] to look with love at those who seem different instead of turning away?

> The priest does not heal, does not provide a prognosis; this is not about medicine or sickness. It is about noticing the details that most of us prefer to avoid. Leviticus 13 publicly acknowledges that boils, rashes, scabs, and pus are all possible expressions of the human body. . . . As readers of these texts, we are momentarily asked to pay attention, as the priests were required to do. Instead of reading these chapters with disgust or boredom, we might approach them with curiosity and with awe for all the ways that the body can

---

55. Marmon, "Reflections," 232–54.
56. Gafney, *Womanist Midrash*, 113–15.
57. 1 Pet 2:5.

Misreading Ritual

express itself in the course of living and healing. . . . Scabs mean that the body is regenerating itself. This is the stuff of life.[58]

Again, all this requires a great deal of care and discernment. Purity metaphors are highly vulnerable to abuse; they activate some very un-loving aspects of human psychology.[59] We can't tell just one story about ritual impurity—whether that story is based on classification, life and death, or reverence—and expect that story to be appropriate for every situation. But the impurity regulations of Leviticus and Numbers aren't going away, and the more tools we have to interpret them the better. Ritual purity is part of a much larger story: sacrifice and other laws of the Torah, yes, but also the even bigger story of God choosing a people for himself, setting them free and making them holy, and ultimately redeeming the whole world. When we read all of scripture as one big interconnected story, with "how do I love God and love my neighbor even more?" as our guiding question, we'll get much better and richer interpretations.

---

58. Kamionkowski, *Leviticus*, 128–29.
59. Beck, *Unclean*.

8

Food Laws

One major area of Old Testament law has been conspicuously absent from the discussion so far: the dietary restrictions of Leviticus 11 (and Deuteronomy 14). Here we have long lists of criteria for distinguishing between pure and impure land animals, fish, birds, and "swarming things." All these regulations use the language of purity, and there's extensive discussion of how contact with the dead body of an impure creature makes people[1] and even objects[2] ritually impure, with the kinds of cleansing procedures (washing, waiting until evening) that we've come to expect.

But the food laws differ from other ritual impurity regulations in important ways. We've seen that, with very few exceptions, becoming ritually impure isn't forbidden; what's forbidden is going to the sanctuary before you've purified yourself. The food laws, by contrast, are very explicit that eating impure creatures *is not allowed at all*: "these are the [pure] creatures that you may eat;"[3] "of their [impure] flesh you shall not eat, and their carcasses you shall not touch;"[4] "to make a distinction between the unclean and the clean, and between the living creature that may be eaten and the living creature that may not be eaten."[5]

---

1. Lev 11:24–28, 31, 39–40.
2. Lev 11:32–38.
3. Lev 11:2.
4. Lev 11:8.
5. Lev 11:47.

Does this mean we've gotten ritual impurity all wrong? Since impure animals are explicitly forbidden, should we conclude that all the other sources of ritual impurity are implicitly forbidden too? I doubt it; as we saw in chapter 6, there's just too much evidence that becoming ritually impure is common, expected, and not a sin. Instead, this looks like another case where the Old Testament's guidelines for life with God break out of the neat categories we try to put them in. There are very real differences between what we've been calling "ritual impurity" and what we've been calling "moral impurity," but the fact that they're different doesn't mean they're the only two possible ways things can work. The food laws are a little bit of both, not clearly one or the other.[6]

There is, of course, something else that the food laws have in common with ordinary ritual impurity regulations: there's a long history of interpreting both as rules for promoting health. In modern times, a popular explanation for the distinction between pure and impure creatures is that the ones classified as impure carry trichinosis or tularemia.[7] Other commentators argue that shellfish are more likely to carry disease; or that draining the blood, which is liable to carry parasites, has historically made Jews less susceptible to plagues.[8] These ideas have more than a family resemblance to modern proposals that the laws of ritual impurity are really germ theory in disguise, but the idea that the impure animals just aren't good for you is actually very old. Maimonides believes that pork, blood, and other forbidden things are "unwholesome;"[9] Nachmanides argues more specifically that shellfish live in unhealthfully cold waters[10] and that milk from unclean animals harms the reproductive organs and turns children into lepers![11]

But many interpreters find hygienic interpretations of the food laws no more convincing than hygienic interpretations of ritual impurity, and for similar reasons. If the goal was to protect the Israelites from food-borne illnesses, the elaborate lists of Leviticus 11 seem like an inefficient way to go about things. Wouldn't it have been simpler to just require that all meat be thoroughly cooked? Once again, scripture is inviting us to take another look, to explore what else these rules might have to teach us about life with God.

---

6. Klawans, *Impurity and Sin*, 31–32; Willis, *Leviticus*, 102–3, 112–13.
7. Albright, *Yahweh*, 177–78.
8. Hertz, *Pentateuch and Haftorahs*, 448–50.
9. Maimonides, *Guide* 3.48.
10. Nachmanides, *Leviticus* 11:9.
11. Nachmanides, *Leviticus* 11:13.

Food Laws

Discipline and distinctiveness

Dietary restrictions, as anyone knows who has an allergy or who avoids certain foods for religious or ethical or health reasons, aren't always easy to follow. Keeping kosher requires a lot of discipline, and one way to understand the food laws of the Old Testament is to say that this is exactly the point: to follow these detailed regulations, day in and day out, is excellent training in self-control.[12] Philo attributes these restrictions to the fact that pork and shellfish are delicious: abstinence from these enticing foods is a good way to build character.[13] (I'm curious to know whether Philo learned about the superior flavor of pork from personal experience, or whether he relied on his Gentile friends for this information.)

This idea is fine as far as it goes, but it's unsatisfying by itself: *any* set of intrusive restrictions could have served the same purpose. It doesn't matter what the laws are, as long as they're difficult to follow. God could have forbidden any creature that was an odd number of years old, or any female fish, or required the Israelites to eat standing on one foot, and that would have been just as effective. Of course, just because we don't like the reason for a law doesn't mean that wasn't actually the reason for the law; but it seems fair to be a little suspicious of any reading that closes off whole sections of scripture as arbitrary and uninteresting.

And, as it turns out, most commentators go beyond a "because I said so" explanation and identify reasons why *these particular* creatures are singled out as pure or impure. Philo doesn't stop with the self-control explanation; Philo being Philo, he can't resist identifying detailed allegorical meanings for every rule. Fish with fins and scales are strong and can swim against the current, representing temperance; shellfish can't.[14] Insects with jointed legs above the feet are pure because they represent human reason that leaps up from earth to heaven, but creatures with many feet are "slaves of . . . all the passions."[15] Reptiles that crawl on their bellies are like people enslaved to the desire for food;[16] this is also why the entrails of sacrificial animals have to be washed.[17] Alternatively, creatures with no legs represent

---

12. Elliott, *Engaging Leviticus*, 99–103; Hertz, *Pentateuch and Haftorahs*, 449.
13. Philo, *Spec.* 4.101.
14. Philo, *Spec.* 4.110–12.
15. Philo, *Spec.* 4.113–15 (Yonge).
16. Philo, *Spec.* 4.113.
17. Philo, *Migr.* 67.

Misreading Ritual

people who believe in no god, while creatures with many legs represent people who believe in many gods.[18] Chewing the cud represents a man who meditates on the things he has learned, and a cloven hoof represents an understanding of the difference between good and evil;[19] therefore, clean animals must have both characteristics. These last two ideas, comparing chewing the cud to meditation and cloven hooves to distinguishing between good and evil, were especially popular among ancient commentators, both Jewish and Christian,[20] and even have modern advocates.[21]

This allegorical approach is foreign to a lot of modern readers. I don't see any reason to object to symbolic interpretations in general; after all, central Christian practices like baptism and communion get their meaning in part from their symbolism. If eating ruminants reminds you to meditate on God's word, that's great. But although some associations are straightforward enough (birds of prey are off-limits; we, too, should avoid violent and predatory behavior), others seem awfully post-hoc. If the rules had been different, it would have been easy to come up with allegorical explanations going the opposite way: cloven hooves are forbidden because they represent a "double-minded and unstable" man;[22] animals that chew the cud are forbidden because they represent "a fool who reverts to his folly."[23] Not to mention the fact that commentators have come up with wildly varying interpretations of the very same rules! Do fins represent strength to swim against the current, as Philo thinks? Or do they represent the "wings of faith"?[24] Or the contemplative life?[25]

Besides all this, allegorical approaches tend to have a piecemeal character. Not always; for example, Nobuyoshi Kiuchi proposes that the unclean animals represent the serpent of Genesis 3.[26] (I find this idea plausible enough for some of the restrictions, but unconvincing as a comprehensive explanation. Sure, eels seem serpent-like, but lobsters?) More common, though, is an approach like Philo's that gives a different explanation for

---

18. Philo, *Migr.* 69.
19. Philo, *Agr.* 131–33; *Spec.* 4.106–8.
20. Elliott, *Engaging Leviticus*, 104–6; *Let. Aris.* 150–54; Theodoret, *Questions* 11.1.
21. Kiuchi, *Leviticus*, 209.
22. Jas 1:8.
23. Prov 26:11.
24. Theodoret, *Questions* 11.2.
25. Elliott, *Engaging Leviticus*, 107.
26. Kiuchi, *Leviticus*, 204–9.

Food Laws

each forbidden type. The problem is that item-by-item interpretations don't so much explain the food laws as replace one list with another list. Again, the fact that we don't like a certain interpretation or don't find it satisfying doesn't mean the interpretation is wrong. Nor is a diversity of interpretations necessarily bad; chapter 7 has just argued that the ritual purity regulations have multiple overlapping meanings, and for Christians even something as central as baptism represents *both* cleansing from sin[27] *and* participation in the death and resurrection of Jesus[28]—with a connection to the flood as a bonus![29] But there's no harm in continuing to look for an explanation that fits in more clearly with the larger story of scripture.

Before we move on, we should look at one more twist on the idea of dietary laws as discipline. Restrictions on food, which make themselves unavoidably felt in daily life, do more than promote individual self-control; they also contribute to community formation. It's a commonplace observation that keeping kosher has played a significant role in maintaining Jewish identity as a people holy and set apart, even through millennia of exile and dispersion.[30] To suggest that these regulations were at least partly *intended* to create a distinctive people seems reasonable, although to say this is their *only* purpose runs into some of the same problems as the discipline theory (it doesn't matter what the rules are, as long as they're annoying enough).

Of course, dietary restrictions are especially effective at setting a people apart if they're different from what those people's neighbors eat. Some commentators have proposed that this is exactly what Leviticus 11 is trying to do; Aphrahat, for example, argues that Moses "made unclean for them those very things which had been clean for them to eat in the land of Egypt, and he commanded them to eat those very things which they had worshipped in the land of Egypt and of which they had formerly not eaten."[31] Aphrahat specifically claims that Egyptians eat a lot of pork, which would explain why pork is forbidden for Israelites.[32] One problem with this line of reasoning is that it's not clear we have the facts right; Herodotus, by contrast, writes that Egyptians consider pigs unclean and eat them only

---

27. Acts 22:16.
28. Rom 6:3–4.
29. 1 Pet 3:20–21.
30. Hertz, *Pentateuch and Haftorahs*, 448.
31. Aphrahat, *Demonstrations* 15.4.
32. Aphrahat, *Demonstrations* 15.3.

on restricted occasions.[33] Of course, Herodotus and Aphrahat were writing centuries apart (Herodotus much earlier), and both were writing long after the time period described in Exodus—basically, it's not clear that ancient writers can give us much in the way of reliable information about the even-more-ancient Egyptians.

A further problem is that ancient Israel had lots of neighbors, and those neighbors had a variety of practices. Probably just about any animal you pick would have been eaten by somebody and forbidden by somebody else. So it's not clear how we could be sure that any particular prohibition was intended to make the Israelites different from these people over here, as opposed to more similar to those people over there. (The theory that certain species were chosen for sacrifice in order to distinguish Israelite worship from their neighbors' is similarly difficult to verify.[34]) All in all, the food laws *in general* have indeed contributed to a distinctive identity for the Jewish people, but we need to look further to understand the specifics.

Categories and creation

Mary Douglas most famously applied her analysis of impurity as matter out of place, discussed in chapter 7, to the dietary regulations of Leviticus 11. Her argument is that the creatures labeled impure are the ones that don't fit neatly into categories. Among larger mammals, for example, "livestock" is the paradigm category (appropriately enough for a pastoralist society); cud-chewing and split hooves are useful features for identifying clear members of the category (cows, sheep, and goats, but also a few wild species) and excluding marginal cases (pigs, camels, etc.).[35] Acceptable species have to move properly through their element of land, water, or air: shellfish aren't "fishy" enough; some insects walk on four legs like land animals; some animals walk on paws (literally "hands") instead of feet; "swarming" creatures don't clearly fit into the walking, swimming, or flying categories.[36]

Douglas's theory isn't completely unsupported in scripture. Other Old Testament laws prohibit various kinds of mixing:

---

33. Herodotus, *Hist.* 2.47.
34. Albright, *Yahweh*, 177–78; Wenham, *Leviticus*, 166–67.
35. Douglas, *Purity and Danger*, 54–55.
36. Douglas, *Purity and Danger*, 55–57.

Food Laws

> You shall not let your animals breed with a different kind; you shall not sow your field with two kinds of seed; nor shall you put on a garment made of two different materials.[37]

If we interpret rules against mixtures as showing concern for proper category boundaries, we could very well understand the food laws in a similar way. Even with this, though, the mixture interpretation of the food laws is still a bit circular. The category of livestock isn't directly defined in the text; we infer it from the requirements about hooves and chewing the cud, and then we use that inferred category to explain those same requirements. Fins and scales define the category of fish, and the category of fish gives us the requirement of fins and scales. *Any* set of regulations that uses general criteria, as opposed to a list of individual species, could be interpreted this way.

A lot of interpreters today agree that the food laws are more than an arbitrary list of prohibitions, and that we can find systematic meanings in them—even if many interpreters don't necessarily agree with Douglas's specific proposals about what those meanings are. (Even Douglas herself later changed her mind about what the food laws are trying to do, as we'll soon see.) Also, as with sacrifice and ritual purity, the answer to a list of one-off explanations doesn't have to be a single explanation that covers everything; multiple overlapping reasons are just fine, and fit the evidence better anyway.[38]

In fact, the classification motif of Leviticus 11 links all the way back to the creation story in Genesis 1.[39] The theme of separation is a regular refrain in God's activity: he separates the light from the darkness,[40] the waters below from the waters above,[41] and the day from the night.[42] Leviticus 11 summarizes the food laws with the same Hebrew verb:

> This is the law pertaining to land animal and bird and every living creature that moves through the waters and every creature that swarms upon the earth, to *make a distinction* between the unclean and the clean, and between the living creature that may be eaten and the living creature that may not be eaten.[43]

---

37. Lev 19:19.
38. Klawans, "Rethinking Leviticus," 95–96.
39. Davis, *Opening Israel's Scriptures*, 69–70.
40. Gen 1:4.
41. Gen 1:7.
42. Gen 1:14.
43. Lev 11:46–47, emphasis added.

Leviticus uses the same major categories (land animals, creatures that live in the waters, birds, and "swarming" creatures) as the creation account. And, just as God creates each living thing "according to its kind,"[44] so Leviticus allows and forbids particular species "according to its kind."[45]

More generally, both Leviticus 11 and the early chapters of Genesis agree that God's creation is more than just a resource for humans to exploit however they want.[46] The paradise of Eden was life within limits; God commanded humans *not to eat* from a particular tree.[47] Leviticus 11 takes up the theme that what we eat matters, and that sometimes God says "no." Day by day, meal by meal, these rules remind God's people that they live in his good world, and that it's proper to honor the good things God has made in all their variety. God, not humankind, is the lord of creation; our use of it ought to be subject to the boundaries he puts in place.

Respect for all life

The dietary laws of Leviticus 11 regulate only animals, not plants. In fact, in the entire Old Testament there's only one law that regulates eating plants: fruit can't be harvested until the tree is at least five years old.[48] This focus on animals suggests that the regulations in this passage are about more than just food, and even about more than just creation; they force us to think about the practice of eating meat, which involves killing a living creature.

Scripture as a whole actually exhibits a profound ambivalence about eating meat. The fact that God gives humans permission to eat meat only after the flood[49] can be, and has been, interpreted as a concession to human violence: "Kill if you must, but let it be animals, not other humans, that you kill."[50] This is hardly an enthusiastic endorsement of eating meat![51] Sure enough, the laws later on put severe restrictions on eating animals, but almost none on eating plants.

44. Gen 1:12, 21, 25.
45. Lev 11:14–16, 19, 22, 29.
46. Davis, "Identity and Eating," 11.
47. Gen 2:15–17.
48. Lev 19:23–25.
49. Gen 9:2–6.
50. Sacks, *Leviticus*, 160.
51. Milgrom, *Leviticus 1–16*, 705–6.

This perspective on the dietary regulations brings us back one more time to Leviticus 17, the explanation that blood makes atonement because "the life of the flesh is in the blood:"

> If anyone of the house of Israel or of the aliens who reside among them eats any blood, I will set my face against that person who eats blood, and will cut that person off from the people. For the life of the flesh is in the blood; and I have given it to you for making atonement for your lives on the altar; for, as life, it is the blood that makes atonement.[52]

This statement isn't part of the first seven chapters of Leviticus with the rest of the instructions about sacrifices. It's not part of the discussion of the Day of Atonement in Leviticus 16. Instead, we find it in the middle of a chapter that puts limit after limit on meat consumption: Domestic animals can't be eaten unless they're brought to the sanctuary and offered as a *shelamim*.[53] Wild animals can be hunted, but the hunter has to drain the animal's blood and cover it with earth.[54] Blood can't be eaten at all. *This* is how we learn that blood represents life—and life is not cheap.

This passage refers in a general way to atonement "on the altar;" it doesn't specify a particular kind of sacrifice. However, the immediate context deals with the *shelamim*. Jacob Milgrom observes that Leviticus 17 is the only passage in the Old Testament that associates atonement with the *shelamim*; the major descriptions in Leviticus 3 and 7 say nothing whatsoever about atonement. He argues that the atonement of Leviticus 17 isn't for sin in general, but for the specific sin of killing an animal.[55] The *shelamim* is the only sacrifice that the worshipper eats, and both this passage[56] and Genesis[57] equate improperly killing an animal with murder. Although Milgrom believes this passage deals *only* with the *shelamim*, my inclination is to let it shed light on all kinds of sacrifices —it helps us understand why sacrificial blood has the cleansing function that it does, and Milgrom's compelling analysis shows the connection between the *shelamim* and the food laws.

---

52. Lev 17:10–11.
53. Lev 17:3–9.
54. Lev 17:13.
55. Milgrom, *Leviticus 1–16*, 704–13.
56. Lev 17:3–4.
57. Gen 9:3–5.

Misreading Ritual

Douglas's later work adopts a similar kind of approach: she sees the restrictions as protective of the creatures they forbid, not expressions of disgust. She compares the fact that only a few species of large land animals are actually permitted as food to the way Israel is chosen as God's particular people,[58] and suggests that swarming creatures represent the fertility God intends for all of creation.[59] Again, not all of the details are convincing; I don't really buy that shellfish need special consideration because they lack the protective scales that regular fish have.[60] (They're called *shell*fish for a reason!) But the general idea that these regulations serve to limit humans' access to the animal kingdom is sound, and we've seen that scripture gives us several ways to get there.

And the laws of Leviticus 11 aren't the only way scripture accomplishes this goal. The sacrifices, in their own way, do the same thing[61]—as one of the few legitimate opportunities for most people to eat meat, sacrifices limit how much meat is eaten and mandate that the animal's life be ritually returned to God when it does happen. Once again, we see that ritual doesn't have to be a dead letter; it's a way to act out lofty principles in physical, bodily form.

> Why a ritual? Could not the Bible have acted in a more ideological way, defined its concept of reverence for life and then left each individual free to live by it without the encumbering restrictions? The answer . . . is that ideals are just abstractions, which humans may pay lip service to yet rarely actualize. All religions urge reverence for life though few adherents live by it. . . .
>
> A ritual, then? Yes, if it is to discipline. So frequent? Yes, if it is to sanctify the home. So tedious? Persistent rain makes holes in rocks.[62]

Let's give Peter a break

Everybody loves to give the apostle Peter a hard time, and usually for good reason. But there's one story where I think he deserves more credit than we tend to give him. In the earliest years of the church, as the little group of

---

58. Douglas, *Leviticus as Literature*, 148–49.
59. Douglas, *Leviticus as Literature*, 159–63.
60. Douglas, *Leviticus as Literature*, 168–69.
61. Davis, *Opening Israel's Scriptures*, 66–67.
62. Milgrom, *Leviticus 1–16*, 736.

Food Laws

Jesus-followers is trying to figure out what their community needs to look like, Peter has a strange vision:

> [Peter] saw the heaven opened and something like a large sheet coming down, being lowered to the ground by its four corners. In it were all kinds of four-footed creatures and reptiles and birds of the air. Then he heard a voice saying, "Get up, Peter; kill and eat." But Peter said, "By no means, Lord; for I have never eaten anything that is profane or unclean." The voice said to him again, a second time, "What God has made clean, you must not call profane." This happened three times, and the thing was suddenly taken up to heaven.[63]

Gentile Christians, especially those of us who have no experience keeping kosher, see yet another example of Peter being stubborn and not a little dense. Of course Peter, as a devout Jew, would be used to avoiding impure animals. But the reason not to eat them is because God said so; here Peter has *a direct command from God* to do something different, and you would think Peter would recognize God's authority to change the rules. Besides, Peter just spent several years following a teacher who radically re-prioritized certain thinking about purity practices (remember Mark 7?), someone he now recognizes as the Messiah. So what's the big deal?

In the end, the story turns out not to be about food laws at all (although food was a major issue in the early church, and one that was surely lurking in the background as readers of Acts re-told this story). Rather, the vision is preparing Peter to preach to the first Gentile converts; the unclean animals are a symbol of the Gentiles who are now to be included in God's people. But Peter doesn't know that during the vision itself; while it's happening, as far as he's concerned, it is very much about food. And if we want to be fair to Peter, we have to recognize that this was in fact a *very* big deal.

Following dietary restrictions, and avoiding pork in particular, was well established as a distinctive Jewish practice. Around the same time period as Peter's vision, Philo joined a diplomatic delegation of Alexandrian Jews to the Roman emperor Caligula, asking him to stop trying to have statues of himself erected in synagogues and the temple. (Also, Alexandrian Jews had been driven into ghettos by their enemies and massacred.[64] The mission was an extremely serious one.) Not only did they get an insulting reception—Caligula kept interrupting their presentation, running around

---

63. Acts 10:11–16.
64. Philo, *Legat.* 119–31.

the site of an upcoming festival and giving orders about how to decorate it—but their opponents openly made fun of them for not eating pork.[65]

And faithful Jews experienced more than just mockery; there had already been certain times and places where staying faithful to those laws was a powerful symbol of Jewish identity. The tyrant Antiochus, whose defeat is commemorated at Chanukkah, tried to outlaw Jewish customs just two hundred years earlier. Out of that persecution came stories about heroic Jews who refused to betray God's law even in the face of torture and death:

> Eleazar, one of the scribes in high position, a man now advanced in age and of noble presence, was being forced to open his mouth to eat swine's flesh. But he, welcoming death with honor rather than life with pollution, went up to the rack of his own accord, spitting out the flesh, as all ought to go who have the courage to refuse things that it is not right to taste, even for the natural love of life.
>
> Those who were in charge of that unlawful sacrifice took the man aside because of their long acquaintance with him, and privately urged him to bring meat of his own providing, proper for him to use, and to pretend that he was eating the flesh of the sacrificial meal that had been commanded by the king, so that by doing this he might be saved from death, and be treated kindly on account of his old friendship with them. But making a high resolve, worthy of his years and the dignity of his old age and the gray hairs that he had reached with distinction and his excellent life even from childhood, and moreover according to the holy God-given law, he declared himself quickly, telling them to send him to Hades.[66]

Another story tells how seven brothers made the same choice Eleazar did and were tortured to death one after another—encouraged, and followed, by their mother.[67]

In this context, I frankly don't blame Peter at all. If God is saying, "Oh, never mind about that whole kosher thing," then did Eleazar die for nothing? I imagine Peter might have felt the way a proud veteran in our time might feel. If your friends died for their country, doesn't it dishonor their memory to burn the flag?

65. Philo, *Legat.* 361–66.
66. 2 Macc 6:18–23.
67. 2 Macc 7.

Food Laws

This doesn't mean that a heroic sacrifice puts an end to all future discussion. It's possible to die nobly for a bad cause. It's also possible to die nobly for a good cause, and later the situation changes so that the specific principle in question needs to be honored in a different way. The early church did eventually conclude that Gentile converts don't have to keep all the laws of the Torah in order to follow Jesus. But we can recognize this while *also* appreciating Peter's perspective. If Peter had spent his life expressing faithfulness to God in part through what he ate, then of course changing those rules would be a serious matter—we should expect nothing less! Similarly, the apocryphal book of 2 Maccabees tells yet another martyrdom story in which two Jewish mothers are killed, along with their babies, for having those babies circumcised.[68] I can only imagine how admirers of those women must have felt when they heard the apostle Paul say that "circumcision is nothing, and uncircumcision is nothing."[69] There's a reason Paul had to work so hard to convince churches that it was okay for Gentiles to stay Gentiles, and that reason was more than just stubbornness.

What we've said here about the food laws could apply equally well to sacrifices or to ritual purity. It's easy for Christians who don't do these things to make light of the early church and its struggles to figure out how followers of Jesus should live. If the laws of the Old Testament were more than "because God said so"—if they were meaningful and life-giving in their own right—then Jews of that time shouldn't have been waiting to jump at the first chance to abandon them. And indeed they weren't. The early church eventually expressed the life-honoring, community-forming goals of Leviticus 11 in a different way, by including Gentiles as part of God's distinctive people; but this doesn't mean that those principles never mattered, or that diet was a silly way to live them out. Christians who want to learn more deeply what God is like should be willing to spend some time in the world of Torah, to honor the God who revealed himself first in the Old Testament and the many faithful worshippers who have found him there.

---

68. 2 Macc 6:10.
69. 1 Cor 7:19.

9

BROTHERS, WHAT SHALL WE DO?

WELL, WHAT NOW? SHORT of going out and offering an actual animal sacrifice (which I do not recommend), does any of this have practical significance for Christians today? Or is this whole discussion a series of "stupid controversies, genealogies, dissensions, and quarrels about the law"?[1] Shouldn't we be focusing on the core of the Christian faith instead?

In one sense, probably yes. A proper theology of sacrifice isn't central to following Jesus, by any stretch of the imagination. When Jesus was asked which is the greatest commandment, he didn't object to the question and insist that all the commandments are equally valuable; he confidently cited "You shall love the Lord your God with all your heart, and with all your soul, and with all your mind" and "You shall love your neighbor as yourself."[2] Not a word about sacrifices.

But I don't believe this means we should cut those two verses out of our Bibles and throw the rest away. Jesus ministered to the sick, but he also found time for theological discussions about worship[3] and purity.[4] The things we say about God really do matter. I believe there are several ways that a positive, edifying theology of these "ritual" laws can lead us back to loving God and loving neighbor.

---

1. Titus 3:9.
2. Matt 22:34–40.
3. John 4:19–24.
4. Mark 7:1–23.

First, God isn't out to make us miserable. Some Christian distortions of these laws—the idea that sacrifice was a perpetual guilt trip, that ritual purity was legalistic and empty, that the whole system was meant to wear people down in preparation for Jesus—are all too similar to the tired old trope of an angry Old Testament God contrasted with a loving New Testament God. A better theology sees the same God revealed in *both* testaments: one who loves his people so much that he condescends to meet them in all kinds of ways, sacrifice included. Moreover, when we say that sacrifice was not about punishing animals for human sin, that doesn't mean we sweep sin under the rug. On the contrary, a richer understanding of how the sacrificial system *actually* deals with sin lets us see sin for what it really is. Sin is more than just individual guilt for discrete wrong actions. It's that too, but it's *also* a pollution that infects the human community and even creation itself. Sacrifices help people join the hard work of dealing with sin: confessing, repenting, cleansing, and making amends. And sacrifices also picture the ultimate goal of dealing with sin: community with God and with each other.

Second, these laws encourage, and even demand, embodied holy living. For Christians whose encounters with God trend towards the cerebral, a worship practice like sacrifice is shockingly physical. (Depending on our specific traditions, some of us would do well to explore more embodied forms of worship.) The regulations around ritual purity make this point even more strongly: to follow them requires loving attention to the bodies God has given us. Without literalistically trying to import identical practices into our alien culture, Christians today can still be inspired by these laws to revere the many kinds of bodies God chose to create. How can we show reverence for those who are old or disabled in a culture that worships youth, strength, and a narrow definition of beauty? How can we choose the foods we eat in a way that glorifies God and honors his creation?

Finally, treating sacrifice as a bizarre and incomprehensible practice—one that was forced on reluctant humans by a strange God—demonstrates a remarkable degree of cultural blindness. Animal sacrifice has been far more common, even in recent times, than many western Christians realize. Dismissing the whole thing is very unloving to our neighbors in other cultures who practice animal sacrifice now, or whose communities have practiced it in living memory. This doesn't mean we have to endorse any and all sacrificial practices. But there's a difference between debating whether literal sacrifice is appropriate in a given context, and starting from the assumption that no reasonable person could find spiritual meaning in a sacrifice. Moses and David encountered God through sacrifice; why should we be surprised when our brothers and sisters do the same today?[5] Of course, the details of sacrifice are different in every culture, and we don't expect modern sacrifices to correspond exactly to what's described in Leviticus. (Nor, in a missional context, do we expect non-Christian sacrificial practices to map neatly onto the biblical system.[6]) But those of us who have never practiced sacrifice in any form have a lot to learn from those who have.[7]

The "ritual" laws of Leviticus invite us into a real, messy, and inescapably physical life of holiness. When we make faith a purely spiritual thing, when we disdain using our bodies to act out the drama of life with God, we're denying the value of incarnation. Christians who claim to follow Jesus put their trust in a God who dove headfirst into his own creation. In a culture where faith is all too often disembodied, may the book of Leviticus guide us to follow Jesus' lead into a life where God intends for all of his creation to flourish.

---

5. Britt, "Ritual Struggle," 1–26; Kane, "Ritual Formation," 386–410.
6. Behera, "Mizo Beliefs," 39–53; Wong, "Notion of כפר," 77–95.
7. Davis, *Opening Israel's Scriptures*, 65–66.

Bibliography

Albo, Joseph. *Book of Principles (Sefer Ha-'Ikkarim)*. Translated by Isaac Husik. The Schiff Library of Jewish Classics 3. Philadelphia: Jewish Publication Society of America, 1946.

Albright, William Foxwell. *Yahweh and the Gods of Canaan: A Historical Analysis of Two Contrasting Faiths*. Garden City, NY: Anchor, 1969.

Amin, C. R. "Hinduism and Its Influence on Health Education." *Health Education Journal* 17 (1959) 58–62.

Aphrahat. *Demonstrations*. In *Aphrahat and Judaism: The Christian-Jewish Argument in Fourth-Century Iran*, translated by Jacob Neusner. Leiden: Brill, 1971.

Apollonius of Rhodes. *Argonautica*. Translated by Edward P. Coleridge. London: George Bell & Sons, 1889.

Assohoto, Barnabe and Samuel Ngewa. "Genesis." In *Africa Bible Commentary*, edited by Tokunboh Adeyemo, 9–84. Grand Rapids: Zondervan, 2006.

Attridge, Harold W. "Pollution, Sin, Atonement, Salvation." In *Religions of the Ancient World: A Guide*, edited by Sarah Iles Johnston, 71–83. Cambridge: The Belknap Press of Harvard University Press, 2004.

Beck, Richard. *Stranger God: Meeting Jesus in Disguise*. Minneapolis: Fortress, 2017.

———. *Unclean: Meditations on Purity, Hospitality, and Mortality*. Eugene, OR: Cascade, 2011.

Behera, Marina Ngursangzeli. "Mizo Beliefs and the Christian Gospel: Their Interaction with Reference to the Concepts of Health and Healing." *Studies in World Christianity* 20 (2014) 39–53.

Bell, Rob. "Blood, Guts, & Fire: The Gospel according to Leviticus." https://robbell.com/portfolio/leviticus/.

Booth, Roger P. *Jesus and the Laws of Purity: Tradition History and Legal History in Mark 7*. JSNTSup 13. Sheffield: JSOT, 1986.

Borg, Marcus J. *Conflict, Holiness, and Politics in the Teachings of Jesus*. New ed. London: Continuum, 1998.

———. *Jesus in Contemporary Scholarship*. Harrisburg, PA: Trinity, 1994.

Brenz, Johannes. *In Leviticum Librum Mosi Commentarius*. Frankfurt: Peter Brubach, 1562.

Britt, Samuel I. "'Sacrifice Honors God': Ritual Struggle in a Liberian Church." *JAAR* 76 (2008) 1–26.

Bibliography

Brown, Raymond E. *The Gospel According to John 1–12*. Vol. 1 of *The Gospel According to John*. AB 29. Garden City, NY: Doubleday, 1966.

Büchsel, Friedrich. "ἱλάσκομαι, ἱλασμός B–E." In *TDNT* 3:310–18.

Calvin, John. *Institutes of the Christian Religion*. Translated by Ford Lewis Battles. LCC 20–21. 2 vols. Philadelphia: Westminster, 1960.

Chingota, Felix. "Leviticus." In *Africa Bible Commentary*, edited by Tokunboh Adeyemo, 129–68. Grand Rapids: Zondervan, 2006.

Choksy, Jamsheed K. *Purity and Pollution in Zoroastrianism: Triumph over Evil*. Austin: University of Texas Press, 1989.

Chytraeus, David. *On Sacrifice: A Reformation Treatise in Biblical Theology*. Translated by John Warwick Montgomery. St. Louis: Concordia, 1962.

Cohen, Shaye J. D. "Menstruants and the Sacred in Judaism and Christianity." In *Women's History and Ancient History*, edited by Sarah B. Pomeroy, 273–99. Chapel Hill: University of North Carolina Press, 1991.

———. "Purity and Piety: The Separation of Menstruants from the Sancta." In *Daughters of the King: Women and the Synagogue: A Survey of History, Halakhah, and Contemporary Realities*, edited by Susan Grossman and Rivka Haut, 103–15. Philadelphia: Jewish Publication Society of America, 1992.

Cowley, A., ed. and trans. *Aramaic Papyri of the Fifth Century BC*. Osnabruck: Zeller, (1923) 1967.

Crossan, John Dominic. *Jesus: A Revolutionary Biography*. San Francisco: Harper SanFrancisco, 1994.

Davis, Ellen F. "Identity and Eating: A Christian Reading of Leviticus." *Studies in Christian Ethics* 30 (2017) 3–14.

———. *Opening Israel's Scriptures*. Oxford: Oxford University Press, 2019.

Derrett, J. Duncan M. *Law in the New Testament*. London: Darton, Longman & Todd, 1970.

Dhirasekera, Jothiya. "Some Observations on the Health Education Content of Buddhism." *Health Education Journal* 17 (1959) 63–65.

The Didascalia Apostolorum in Syriac. Translated by Arthur Vööbus. Vol. 2. Corpus Scriptorum Christianorum Orientalium 408. Leuven: Secrétariat du CorpusSCO, 1979.

Douglas, Mary. *Leviticus as Literature*. Oxford: Oxford University Press, 2000.

———. *Purity and Danger: An Analysis of Concepts of Pollution and Taboo*. London: Routledge, 1966.

El Bedri, Khalafalla Babiker. "Health Education and Islam." *Health Education Journal* 17 (1959) 79–88.

Eilberg-Schwartz, Howard. *The Savage in Judaism: An Anthropology of Israelite Religion and Ancient Judaism*. Bloomington: Indiana University Press, 1990.

Elliott, Mark W. *Engaging Leviticus: Reading Leviticus Theologically with Its Past Interpreters*. Eugene, OR: Cascade, 2012.

Evans, Rachel Held. *A Year of Biblical Womanhood: How a Liberated Woman Found Herself Sitting on Her Roof, Covering Her Head, and Calling Her Husband "Master."* Nashville: Nelson, 2012.

Ferguson, Everett. *Backgrounds of Early Christianity*. 3rd ed. Grand Rapids: Eerdmans, 2003.

Bibliography

Fonrobert, Charlotte Elisheva. "Judaizers, Jewish Christians, and Others." In *The Jewish Annotated New Testament*, edited by Amy-Jill Levine and Marc Zvi Brettler, 637–40. 2nd ed. Oxford: Oxford University Press, 2017.

———. *Menstrual Purity: Rabbinic and Christian Reconstructions of Biblical Gender*. Contraversions: Jews and Other Differences. Stanford, CA: Stanford University Press, 2000.

Fredriksen, Paula. "Did Jesus Oppose the Purity Laws?" *BRev* 11 (1995) 19–25, 42–48.

Frymer-Kensky, Tikva. "Pollution, Purification, and Purgation in Biblical Israel." In *The Word of the Lord Shall Go Forth: Essays in Honor of David Noel Freedman in Celebration of His Sixtieth Birthday*, edited by Carol L. Myers and M. O'Connor, 399–414. ASOR Special Volume Series 1. Winona Lake, IN: Eisenbrauns, 1983.

Gafney, Wilda C. *Womanist Midrash: A Reintroduction to the Women of the Torah and the Throne*. Louisville: Westminster John Knox, 2017.

Gane, Roy E. *Altar Call*. Berrien Springs, MI: Diadem, 1999.

———. *Cult and Character: Purification Offerings, Day of Atonement, and Theodicy*. Winona Lake, IN: Eisenbrauns, 2005.

———. *Old Testament Law for Christians: Original Context and Enduring Application*. Grand Rapids: Baker Academic, 2017.

———. "Privative Preposition מן in Purification Offering Pericopes and the Changing Face of 'Dorian Gray.'" *JBL* 127 (2008) 209–22.

Ganz, Nancy E. *Leviticus*. 2nd rev. Herein Is Love 3. Wapwallopen, PA: Shepherd, 2002.

Girard, René. *Violence and the Sacred*. Translated by Patrick Gregory. Baltimore: Johns Hopkins University Press, 1977.

Goldingay, John. "Old Testament Sacrifice and the Death of Christ." In *Atonement Today: A Symposium at St. John's College, Nottingham*, edited by John Goldingay, 1–20. London: SPCK, 1995.

Gregory the Great. *Selected Epistles of Gregory the Great, Bishop of Rome: Books 9–14*. Vol. 13 of *NPNF*2. Translated by James Barmby.

Grotius, Hugo. *Annotata ad Vetus Testamentum*. 2 vols. Paris: Sebastiani & Gabrielis Cramoisy, 1644.

Gruber, Mayer I. "Purity and Impurity in Halakic Sources and Qumran Law." In *Wholly Woman, Holy Blood: A Feminist Critique of Purity and Impurity*, edited by Kristin De Troyer et al., 65–76. SAC. Harrisburg, PA: Trinity, 2003.

Gurney, O. R. *The Hittites*. Rev. ed. Baltimore: Penguin, 1964.

Hamerton-Kelly, Robert G. *The Gospel and the Sacred: Poetics of Violence in Mark*. Minneapolis: Fortress, 1994.

Harrington, Hannah K. *The Impurity Systems of Qumran and the Rabbis: Biblical Foundations*. SBLDS 143. Atlanta: Scholars, 1993.

Heraclitus. *Heraclitus: Greek Text with a Short Commentary*. Translated by M. Marcovich. Merida: Los Andes University Press, 1967.

Herodotus. *The Histories*. Translated by Robin Waterfield. Oxford World's Classics. Oxford: Oxford University Press, 1998.

Hertz, J. H., ed. and trans. *The Pentateuch and Haftorahs: Hebrew Text, English Translation, and Commentary*. 2nd ed. London: Soncino, 1960.

Homer. *The Iliad*. Translated by Barry B. Powell. Oxford: Oxford University Press, 2013.

Hugh of St. Cher. *In Libros Genesis, Exodi, Levitici, Numeri, Deuteronomii, Josue, Judicum, Ruth, Regum IV, Paralipomenon II, Esdrae IV, Tobiae, Judith, Esther, et Job*, vol. 1 of *In Universum Vetus et Novum Testamentum*. Venice: Nicolaus Pezzana, 1703.

Bibliography

Ibn Ezra, Abraham ben Meir. *Leviticus*, vol. 3 of *Commentary on the Pentateuch*. Translated by H. Norman Strickman and Arthur M. Silver. New York: Menorah, 1988.

Jacobs, A. J. *The Year of Living Biblically: One Man's Humble Quest to Follow the Bible as Literally as Possible*. New York: Simon & Schuster, 2007.

John Chrysostom. *Discourses against Judaizing Christians*. Translated by Paul W. Harkins. The Fathers of the Church: A New Translation 68. Washington, DC: Catholic University of America Press, 1979.

Josephus. *Judean War 2*, vol. 1B of *Flavius Josephus: Translation and Commentary*. Translated by Steve Mason. Leiden: Brill, 2008.

———. *The New Complete Works of Josephus*. Translated by William Whiston. Rev. and exp. ed. Grand Rapids: Kregel, 1999.

Justin Martyr. *Dialogue with Trypho*. Translated by Thomas B. Falls. Revised by Thomas P. Halton. Selections from the Fathers of the Church 3. Washington, DC: Catholic University of America Press, 2003.

Kalas, David. *The Gospel According to Leviticus: Finding God's Love in God's Law*. Nashville: Abingdon, 2019.

Kamionkowski, S. Tamar. *Leviticus*. Wisdom Commentary 3. Collegeville, MN: Liturgical, 2018.

Kane, Ross. "Ritual Formation of Peaceful Publics: Sacrifice and Syncretism in South Sudan (1991–2005)." *Journal of Religion in Africa* 44 (2014): 386–410.

Kiuchi, Nobuyoshi. *Leviticus*. ApOTC 3. Downers Grove, IL: InterVarsity, 2007.

Klawans, Jonathan. *Impurity and Sin in Ancient Judaism*. Oxford: Oxford University Press, 2000.

———. "Notions of Gentile Impurity in Ancient Judaism." *AJSR* 20 (1995) 285–312.

———. *Purity, Sacrifice, and the Temple: Symbolism and Supersessionism in the Study of Ancient Judaism*. Oxford: Oxford University Press, 2005.

———. "Rethinking Leviticus and Rereading 'Purity and Danger.'" *AJSR* 27 (2003) 89–102.

———. "Something Bigger than Girard." *BSR* 45 (2016) 23–27.

Krakowski, Eve. "Maimonides' Menstrual Reform in Egypt." *JQR* 110 (2020) 245–89.

Lambert, W. G. *Babylonian Oracle Questions*. MC 13. Winona Lake, IN: Eisenbrauns, 2007.

Landry, Ed. *Light in the Shadows: Making Sense of the Old Testament Law, Priests, Sacrifices and Feasts*. An Easy-to-Understand Bible Commentary. Nashville: Uplifting Christian, 2017.

LeClerc, Jean. *Mosis Prophetae Libri Quatuor: Exodus, Leviticus, Numeri, et Deuteronomium*. New exp. and rev. ed. Amsterdam: Henricum Schelte, 1693.

Leichty, E. "Ritual, 'Sacrifice,' and Divination in Mesopotamia." In *Ritual and Sacrifice in the Ancient Near East: Proceedings of the International Conference Organized by the Katholieke Universiteit Leuven from the 17th to the 20th of April 1991*, edited by J. Quaegebeur, 237–42. Leuven: Uitgeverij Peeters & Departement Oriëntalistiek Leuven, 1993.

The Letter of Aristeas. Translated by Benjamin G. Wright III. CEJL. Berlin: De Gruyter, 2015.

Levine, Amy-Jill. "Knowing and Preaching the Jewish Jesus." *ChrCent* (March 2019). https://www.christiancentury.org/article/interview/knowing-and-preaching-jewish-jesus.

Bibliography

Levine, Baruch A. *The JPS Torah Commentary: Leviticus*. Philadelphia: Jewish Publication Society of America, 1989.

Levy, David M. *The Tabernacle: Shadows of the Messiah: Its Sacrifices, Services, and Priesthood*. Grand Rapids: Kregel, (1993) 2003.

The Life Book. Mark ed. Nashville, TN: The Gideons International, 2017.

Lucian. *Sacrifices*. In *Lucian*. Translated by A. M. Harmon. 8 vols. London: Heinemann, 1921.

Maccoby, Hyam. *Ritual and Morality: The Ritual Purity System and Its Place in Judaism*. Cambridge: Cambridge University Press, 1999.

———. "Statutes That Were Not Good (Ezekiel 20:25–26): Traditional Interpretations." *Journal of Textual Reasoning* 8.1 (1999).

Maimonides. *The Book of Cleanness*. Vol. 10 of *The Code of Maimonides (Mishneh Torah)*. Translated by Herbert Danby. YJS 8. New Haven: Yale University Press, 1954.

———. *The Guide of the Perplexed*. Translated by M. Friedländer. 3 vols. New York: Hebrew, 1885.

Malina, Bruce J. *The New Testament World: Insights from Cultural Anthropology*. Atlanta: John Knox, 1981.

Marmon, Naomi. "Reflections on Contemporary *Miqveh* Practice." In *Women and Water: Menstruation in Jewish Life and Law*, edited by Rahel R. Wasserfall, 232–54. Brandeis Series on Jewish Women. Hanover, NH: University Press of New England, 1999.

McCarthy, Dennis J. "The Symbolism of Blood and Sacrifice." *JBL* 88 (1969) 166–76.

Meachem, Tirzah. "An Abbreviated History of the Development of the Jewish Menstrual Laws." In *Women and Water: Menstruation in Jewish Life and Law*, edited by Rahel R. Wasserfall, 23–39. Brandeis Series on Jewish Women. Hanover, NH: University Press of New England, 1999.

Milgrom, Jacob. "Israel's Sanctuary: The Priestly 'Picture of Dorian Gray.'" *RB* 83 (1976) 390–99.

———. *Leviticus 1–16*. Vol. 1 of *Leviticus*. AB 3. New York: Doubleday, 1991.

Modi, Jivanji Jamshedji. *The Religious Ceremonies and Customs of the Parsees*. Mumbai: British India, 1922.

Morales, L. Michael. *Who Shall Ascend the Mountain of the Lord? A Biblical Theology of the Book of Leviticus*. New Studies in Biblical Theology 37. Downers Grove, IL: InterVarsity, 2015.

Morrow, William S. *An Introduction to Biblical Law*. Grand Rapids: Eerdmans, 2017.

Mouton, Alice. "Animal Sacrifice in Hittite Anatolia." In *Animal Sacrifice in the Ancient Greek World*, edited by Sarah Hitch and Ian Rutherford, 239–52. Cambridge: Cambridge University Press, 2017.

Nachmanides. *Leviticus*. Vol. 3 of *Commentary on the Torah*. Translated by Charles B. Chavel. New York: Shilo, 1974.

Neusner, Jacob. "The Fellowship (חבורה) in the Second Jewish Commonwealth." *HTR* 53 (1960) 125–42.

———, trans. *Introduction, Vayyiqra Dibura Denedabah, and Vayyiqra Dibura Dehobah*. Vol. 1 of *Sifra: An Analytical Translation*. BJS 138. Atlanta: Scholars, 1988.

———, trans. *Ketubot*. Vol. 22 of *The Talmud of the Land of Israel: A Preliminary Translation and Explanation*. Chicago: University of Chicago Press, 1985.

———, trans. *The Later Midrash Compilations: Genesis Rabbah, Leviticus Rabbah, and Pesiqta deRab Kahana*. Vol. 3 of *The Judaism behind the Texts: The Generative Premises of Rabbinic Literature*. SFSHJ 99. Atlanta: Scholars, 1994.

Bibliography

———, trans. *The Mishnah: A New Translation*. New Haven: Yale University Press, 1988.

———, trans. *Second Division: Moed (The Order of Appointed Times)*. Vol. 2 of *The Tosefta*. New York: Ktav, 1981.

Newton, Michael. *The Concept of Purity at Qumran and in the Letters of Paul*. SNTSMS 53. Cambridge: Cambridge University Press, 1985.

Neyrey, Jerome H. "The Idea of Purity in Mark's Gospel." *Semeia* 35 (1986) 91–128.

O'Connor, Anne. "Listening to Tradition." In *Personally Speaking: Women's Thoughts on Women's Issues*, edited by Liz Steiner-Scott, 74–92. Dublin: Attic, 1985.

Packer, J. I. *Knowing God*. Downers Grove, IL: InterVarsity, 1973.

Parker, Robert. *Miasma: Pollution and Purification in Early Greek Religion*. Oxford: Clarendon, 1983.

———. "Pleasing Thighs: Reciprocity in Greek Religion." In *Reciprocity in Ancient Greece*, edited by Christopher Gill, Norman Postlethwaite, and Richard Seaford, 105–125. Oxford: Oxford University Press, 1998.

Philo. *The Works of Philo*. Translated by C. D. Yonge. New updated ed. Peabody, MA: Hendrickson, 1993.

Pliny the Elder. *Natural History*. Vol. 8: *Books 28–32*. Translated by W. H. S. Jones. LCL. Cambridge: Harvard University Press, 1963.

Poorthuis, Marcel. "Sacrifice as Concession in Christian and Jewish Sources: The *Didascalia Apostolorum* and Rabbinic Literature." In *The Actuality of Sacrifice: Past and Present*, edited by Alberdina Houtman, et al., 170–91. Jewish and Christian Perspectives 28. Leiden: Brill, 2015.

Ralph of Flaix. *In Mysticum Illum Moysi Leviticum Libri*. Marburg: Eucharius Ceruicornus Agrippinas, 1536.

Redman, Matt. "The Heart of Worship." Thankyou Music, 1999.

Regev, Eyal. "Pure Individualism: The Idea of Non-Priestly Purity in Ancient Judaism." *JSJ* 31 (2000) 176–202.

Riskin, Shlomo. *Vayikra: Sacrifice, Sanctity and Silence*. Torah Lights. New Milford, CT: Maggid, 2009.

Rofé, Alexander. *Introduction to the Prophetic Literature*. Translated by Judith H. Seeligmann. Sheffield: Sheffield Academic, 1997.

Roll, Susan K. "The Old Rite of the Churching of Women after Childbirth." In *Wholly Woman, Holy Blood: A Feminist Critique of Purity and Impurity*, edited by Kristin De Troyer et al., 117–41. SAC. Harrisburg, PA: Trinity, 2003.

Ruether, Rosemary Radford. *Faith and Fratricide: The Theological Roots of Anti-Semitism*. New York: Seabury, 1974.

Sacks, Jonathan. *Leviticus: The Book of Holiness*. Covenant & Conversation. New Milford, CT: Maggid & The Orthodox Union, 2015.

Sanders, E. P. *Judaism: Practice and Belief, 63 BCE – 66 CE*. 2nd ed. Minneapolis: Fortress, (1992) 2016.

Selvidge, Marla J. "Mark 5:25–34 and Leviticus 15:19–20: A Reaction to Restrictive Purity Regulations." *JBL* 103 (1984) 619–23.

Simon, Maurice, trans. *The Babylonian Talmud: Seder Zeraʻim*. Vol. of *The Hebrew-English Edition of the Babylonian Talmud*. Edited by Isidore Epstein. London: Soncino, 1948.

Sklar, Jay. *Leviticus: An Introduction and Commentary*. TOTC 3. Downers Grove, IL: InterVarsity, 2014.

Slotki, Israel W., trans. *The Babylonian Talmud: Seder Ṭohoroth*. Vol. of *The Hebrew-English Edition of the Babylonian Talmud*. Edited by Isidore Epstein. London: Soncino, 1948.

Bibliography

Stitskin, Leon D. "A Responsum by Maimonides: Maimonides' Rational Approach to Halakhic Problems." *Tradition: A Journal of Orthodox Jewish Thought* 17.4 (1979) 7–14.

Stowers, Stanley K. "On the Comparison of Blood in Greek and Israelite Ritual." In *Hesed ve-Emet: Studies in Honor of Ernest S. Frerichs*, edited by Jodi Magness and Seymour Gitin, 179–94. BJS 320. Scholars: Atlanta, 1998.

Theodoret. *On Leviticus, Numbers, Deuteronomy, Joshua, Judges, and Ruth.* Vol. 2 of *Theodoret of Cyrus: The Questions on the Octateuch.* Translated by Robert C. Hill. LEC. Washington, DC: Catholic University of America Press, 2007.

Ullucci, Daniel C. *The Christian Rejection of Animal Sacrifice.* Oxford: Oxford University Press, 2012.

Vis, Joshua M. "The Purgation of Persons through the Purification Offering." In *Sacrifice, Cult, and Atonement in Early Judaism and Christianity: Constituents and Critique*, edited by Henrietta L. Wiley and Christian A. Eberhart, 33–57. RBS 85. Atlanta: SBL, 2017.

Waller, James and Mary Edwardsen. "Evolutionism." *ER* 5:214–18.

Wegner, Judith Romney. *Chattel or Person? The Status of Women in the Mishnah.* Oxford: Oxford University Press, 1988.

Wenham, Gordon J. *The Book of Leviticus.* NICOT. Grand Rapids: Eerdmans, 1979.

Willis, Timothy M. *Leviticus.* AOTC. Nashville: Abingdon, 2009.

Witherington, Ben, III. *Women in the Ministry of Jesus: A Study of Jesus' Attitudes to Women and Their Roles as Reflected in His Earthly Life.* SNTSMS 51. Cambridge: Cambridge University Press, 1984.

Wong, Sonia K. "The Notion of כפר in the Book of Leviticus and Chinese Popular Religion." In *Leviticus and Numbers*, edited by Athalya Brenner and Archie Chi Chung Lee, 77–95. Texts @ Contexts. Minneapolis: Fortress, 2013.

Wright, David P. *The Disposal of Impurity: Elimination Rites in the Bible and in Hittite and Mesopotamian Literature.* SBLDS 101. Atlanta: Scholars, 1986.

———. "The Gesture of Hand Placement in the Hebrew Bible and in Hittite Literature." *JAOS* 106 (1986) 433–46.

Wright, N. T. *The Day the Revolution Began: Reconsidering the Meaning of Jesus's Crucifixion.* San Francisco: HarperOne, 2016.

Xenophon. *The Anabasis of Cyrus.* Translated by Wayne Ambler. Ithaca, NY: Cornell University Press, 2007.

General Index

Abraham, 15–16, 32–33, 64, 65
allegorical interpretation
    of food laws, 121–23
    of sacrifices, 65–66
anti-Semitism, 3, 17–18, 24–25
Aphrahat, 2, 123–24
'asham, 41–42, 60–63, 68, 72, 112
atonement, 72–76
    penal substitutionary, 10–11, 14–15, 37–43, 50, 58, 73–75
    with blood, 52
    See also Day of Atonement, *kipper*

blood
    as life, 14, 52–53, 112–13, 127
    as soap, 49–52, 112
    not ritually impure, 111
    prohibition against eating, 52–53, 112–13, 127
burnt offering. See *'olah*

chatta't, 82
    and atonement, 72, 75
    cleansing function of, 46–54, 64, 75, 78, 91, 112
    compared to the *'asham*, 60
    Jesus as, 63, 76
    usually a goat, 76
childbirth, 2, 81–82, 90–91, 95, 96–102, 110, 112, 113
    Christianity and, 100–101
    sex of baby and, 90–91, 101, 110, 117
churching. *See* childbirth: Christianity and
communion. *See* Lord's supper

corpse impurity, 2, 78–79, 83–84, 92, 95, 105, 108–9
    and Jesus, 88
    and severity of impurity, 114–16
    forbidden for high priest, 93
    not sinful, 79, 81–82, 87–89
    social dimensions of, 116
covenant. *See under* sacrifice
creation, 72, 109–10, 124–26

Daniel, 30–31
Day of Atonement, 4, 73, 75, 127
    and exclusion from the sanctuary, 94–95
    and the scapegoat, 39–42
    as spring cleaning, 47–48
Dead Sea Scrolls. *See* Qumran
diet. *See* food laws
divination. *See* sacrifice: as divination
Dorian Gray. *See Picture of Dorian Gray, The*
Douglas, Mary
    on food laws, 124–25, 128
    on ritual impurity, 104, 106–8, 109, 116

evolutionism, 8–12
exile, 1, 45–46, 49, 77, 123
exodus, 1, 16, 17, 24, 77

fellowship offering. See *shelamim*
food laws, 81, 107, 119–31
    and categories, 124–26
    and discipline, 121–23

General Index

(*food laws continued*)
    different from ritual impurity, 119–20
    made obsolete by Jesus, 5, 85–86, 129–31
    See also allegorical interpretation: of food laws; blood: prohibition against eating; hygiene: food laws are not

genital discharges, 2, 112, 116
    consequences of, 92–93, 96–101
    interpretation of, 107, 108–11, 117
    not sinful, 81–82, 88
    uniqueness of, 104–5
    See also menstruation; sex
Girard, René, 10–11
grain offering. *See minchah*
Guide for the Perplexed. *See* Maimonides
guilt offering. *See* '*asham*

hand-leaning, 41–42, 59
Hertz, J. H.
    on food laws, 120, 121, 123
    on sacrifices, 17, 53, 58, 65
hygiene
    food laws are not, 120
    ritual impurity is not, 103–6, 116

Iliad, 31–32, 35
impurity
    moral (*see* moral impurity)
    of animals (*see* food laws)
    ritual (*see* ritual impurity)

Jacob, 16, 33, 73–74
John Chrysostom, 17–18, 25
Josephus, 24–25

kipper, 73–76
Klawans, Jonathan, 85
    on metaphor and symbolism, 50, 72, 113
    on ritual vs. moral impurity, 81, 84, 120
    on the interpretation of impurity, 111, 113, 125

kosher. *See* food laws
law
    as a burden, 1–5, 8
    interpreted by Jesus, 6, 7–8
    respect for, 4, 6–7, 23–25
leprosy. *See* skin disease
Lord's supper, 23, 58
Lucian of Samosata, 9, 13, 32

Maimonides
    on food laws, 120
    on sacrifices, 17, 59
    on ritual impurity, 89–90, 98–99, 114
menstruation, 2, 82, 96–102, 115
    and life and death, 110–11
    Christianity and, 99–100
    consequences of, 92–93, 94–95
    contemporary practices around, 96, 98, 102, 117
    See also genital discharges
mildew. *See* skin disease
Milgrom, Jacob
    on eating meat, 126, 127–28
    on *kipper*, 75
    on pollution caused by sin, 48
    on ritual impurity, 111
    on sacrifices, 30, 41, 47, 61, 70, 71
minchah, 15, 41, 69–71, 72
moral impurity
    cleansed by sacrifices, 42–43
    different from ritual impurity, 81–87, 112–13, 120
Moses, 18, 109
    and food laws, 123
    and sacrifices, 16, 47, 50, 64, 134
music. *See* singing

'*olah*, 20, 34, 68, 71
    function of, 58, 59, 64–67, 72, 112
    specific instances, 15–16
offering of well-being. *See shelamim*

Passover, 6, 24, 25, 72, 77, 94
peace offering. *See shelamim*
penal substitutionary atonement. *See under* atonement

General Index

Philo of Alexandria
   and Caligula, 129–30
   on food laws, 121–23
   on sacrifices, 24, 41, 47, 53–54, 59, 62, 65–66, 70
Picture of Dorian Gray, The, 46–48
prayer, 10, 20
   as an alternative to sacrifice, 17
   ritual impurity and, 93–94, 97–98
purification offering. See *chatta't*
purity. *See under* moral impurity; ritual impurity

Qumran, 23, 84, 93

reparation offering. See *'asham*
ritual impurity, 2, 102–18, 133–34
   and Jesus, 5, 6, 85–87, 95
   cleansing of, 75, 90–91
   consequences of, 82–83, 91–95, 97–102
   different from food laws, 119–20
   different from moral impurity, 81–87, 112–13, 120
   in other cultures, 95
   interpretations of, 106–18
   not forbidden, 6, 79, 81–82, 87–89, 93, 119
   of Gentiles, 85, 115
   quasi-, 93–94
   time spent in, 2, 89, 93, 97, 114
   See also childbirth; corpse impurity; genital discharges; hygiene; menstruation; skin disease

Sabbath, 19
   and Jesus, 6, 7, 85
   for the land, 45–46
sacrifice
   as a burden, 3–4, 18, 21–23, 25, 33
   as a human invention, 15–18
   as a meal, 11, 28–31, 37, 68–69
   as bribery, 9, 31–35, 37
   as divination, 36–37, 62
   attraction of, 7, 19, 20–21, 22–25
   cleansing function of, 47–48, 49–53, 57, 75, 76, 90–91
   inappropriate, 19–21, 23

   instructed by Jesus, 6, 25
   made obsolete by Jesus, 5, 7, 25, 26
   multiple meanings of, 27–28, 57–77
   of children, 2, 16, 21, 46–47
   outside the temple, 71
   removal of sin by (*see* sin: removed by sacrifices)
   to God by Gentiles, 24, 64–65
   to inaugurate a covenant, 15, 32–33
   to other gods, 9, 16–17, 18, 24, 28–29, 30–32, 36, 40, 64–65
   violence of, 10, 11, 26
   See also '*asham*; atonement; *chatta't*; hand-leaning; *minchah*; *'olah*; *shelamim*; *tamid*; vows
scapegoat, 39–42
   See also Girard, René
Septuagint, 69, 74, 80
sex, 82, 93, 95, 96–100, 109, 111
shelamim, 20, 58, 72, 77
   and ritual impurity, 82–83
   as a meal, 67–69, 127
   subtypes of, 71–72
sin
   accidental, 62–63
   as impurity, 45–56
   communal, 45–46, 53
   removed by sacrifices, 3–4, 14–15, 38–43, 49–54, 57–58
   See also atonement; ritual impurity: not forbidden; wrath of God
sin offering. See *chatta't*
singing, 18, 20, 22
skin disease, 2, 81–82, 91, 112
   and Jesus, 6, 25, 88–89
   as punishment, 89–90
   consequences of, 6, 92, 95
   interpretations of, 107, 108–9, 113, 117–18
   See also hygiene: different from ritual impurity

tahor. See ritual impurity
tame'. See ritual impurity
tamid, 72, 76–77
temple, 34, 71
   and Jesus, 7–8, 11, 25, 88
   and ritual impurity, 83–84, 88, 93, 99

General Index

(temple continued)
   and the presence of God, 56
   respect for, 23, 24, 25
   See also *Picture of Dorian Gray, The*;
      ritual impurity: consequences of;
      sacrifice: outside the temple
Torah. *See* law

uncleanness. *See under* moral impurity;
   ritual impurity
vows, 31–32, 33–34

wrath of God, 54–55, 62–63
   See also atonement: penal
      substitutionary

Yom Kippur. *See* Day of Atonement

Zoroastrianism, 95, 99, 104, 111–12, 116

Scripture Index

Genesis

1:4	125
1:7	125
1:12	126
1:14	125
1:21	126
1:25	126
1:28	82
2:15–17	126
2:16–17	112
3	122
4:3–5	15
4:3–4	69–70
8:20	15, 64
8:21–22	33
9:1	82
9:2–6	126
9:3–5	52, 127
12:1–3	33
12:7–8	15
13:18	15
15	15, 16
15:7–21	32
15:9–21	65
22	15–16, 64
22:15–18	32–33
26:25	16
28:13–22	33
31:54–55	16
32:20	73–74
33:20	16
35:1–14	16
35:11	82
46:1	16

Exodus

5:3	16
10:25	64
11–13	24
12:46	77
13:17–18	17
15:1–21	18
18:1	64
18:12	64
21:28–30	73
24:5–8	64
25:17–22	73
25:23–30	29
28:30	37
29:10–14	76
29:19–27	72
29:38–42	72
30:28	64
31:9	64
32:4–6	64
32:30–32	75
34:6	54
35:16	64
38:1	64
40:6	64
40:10	64
40:29	64

Leviticus

1:2	15
1:3	65
1:4	72, 75
1:6	65

Scripture Index

(Leviticus continued)

Reference	Page
1:9	29
1:10	76
2	15, 69–70
3:2	69
3:3–5	67–68
3:8	69
3:9–11	68
3:13	69
3:14–16	68
3:17	69
4:1—5:13	60
4	47, 49
4:3–7	47
4:7	64
4:10	64
4:13–18	47
4:18	64
4:20	72
4:22–25	47
4:25	64
4:26	72
4:27–30	47
4:30	64
4:31	72
4:32	76
4:34	64
4:35	72
5	41
5:14—6:7	60
5:15–16a	60–61
5:15	42, 60
5:17	60, 61
6:2–3	60, 61
6:4–6	61
6:4	61
6:6	42
6:7	72
7:11–21	68
7:11–18	22, 71
7:21	82–83
7:31–36	68
8:2	76
8:14–15	47
8:15	42, 50
8:22–36	72
9:15	76
10:1–2	58
11	119
11:2	119
11:8	119
11:14–16	126
11:19	126
11:22	126
11:24–40	114–15
11:24–28	119
11:29	126
11:31	119
11:32–38	119
11:39–40	119
11:46–47	125–26
11:47	119
12	96
12:2–5	91
12:6	90, 91, 112
12:7–8	75
13–14	89, 109
13:45–46	92
14:1–12	91
14:10–20	112
14:18–31	75
14:36	105
15	96, 104
15:8	104
15:13–15	91, 112
15:15	75
15:18	96
15:19–24	96
15:25–30	91
15:28–30	112
15:30	75
16	39–41, 49
16:3	76
16:6	73
16:9	76
16:10–11	73
16:16–18	73
16:16	46
16:18–19	47
16:19	42
16:20	73
16:21–22	39–40
16:24	73
16:27	73
16:30	73
16:32–34	73

17:3–9	127	31:50	75
17:3–4	53, 127	35:33	46
17:10–11	52, 112, 127		
17:13	127	**Deuteronomy**	
18:5	112–13	6:4	97
18:19	93, 98	12:6–7	68
18:24–28	45	14	119
19:19	124–25	18:10	37
19:23–25	126	18:14	37
19:26	37	23:12–13	104
20:3	46–47	26:14	82–83
20:18	93	27:7	68
21:1–3	87	28:27	90
21:10–11	87, 93	30:16	1–2
22:3–6	83	30:19–20	112–13
22:17–30	22	31–32	18
23:12	64		
23:18	64	**Joshua**	
23:19	76	22:10–29	16
24:5–7	29		
26:31	22	**Judges**	
26:34b–35	45–46	5:1–41	18
		11:30–39	33
Numbers			
5:1–4	92	**1 Samuel**	
5:16–26	83	1:3–7	68
6:13–15	70	1:11	33
6:14	67	2:12–17	19, 58
7	76	7:9–10	64
8:8	76	9:11–24	68
12:9–15	90	13:8–14	19, 33
12:10–12	109	14:41	37
15:1–10	70	15:13–23	33
16:47	75	21:4	96–97
19:2–10	81–82	21:6	29
19:11–13	78–79		
19:14–15	114	**2 Samuel**	
19:16	105	3:29	90
19:18–19	114	6:5	18
19:19–21	81–82	6:18–19	68
23:15	65	15:7–12	33
28:3–8	72	24:16	32
28:15	76	24:18	32
28:22	76		
29:5	76		
29:11	76		
29:16–38	76		

SCRIPTURE INDEX

1 Kings

1:9	68
1:41	68
3:15	68
8:64	68
12:28–33	19
16:32	21
18:26	21
22:43	19, 58

2 Kings

3:27	65
5:26–27	90
10:24	65
12:3	19
14:4	19
15:4	19
15:35	19
16:4	19
16:10–16	37
21:3–5	19

2 Chronicles

26:16–20	58
26:18–19	90
29:3–36	21
29:21–24	76
30:17–20	94
34:8–12	21

Ezra

6:17	76
8:35	76

Job

1:5	64–65

Psalms

1:1	82
5	34
6	34
7	35
9	34
10	35
11	35
12	35
13	35
13:1	21
17	35
18	35
20	34, 35
22	34
25	35
26	34, 35
27	34
27:6	22
28	35
30	34
31	35
35	34, 35
37	35
38	35
39	35
40	34
40:6–10	35
40:6a	22
40:8	22
41	35
43	34
43:4	22
44	35
50	21
50:9–13	30
51:10	80
51:16–17	22
52	34
54	34
54:6	22
55	35
56	34
56:12	22
57	34
58	35
59	35
60	35
61	34
62	35
64	35
65:3	74
66	34
66:13–15	22, 34
66:16–18	34
69	34

69:30–31	35
70	35
71	34
73	35
74	35
77	35
79	35
80	35
82:1–3	55
82:8	55
83	35
85	35
86	35
90	35
94	35
98:4–9	54–55
102	34
106	1
107	34
109	34
116	34
116:17	22
118	34
119	4, 35
121	35
123	35
130	35
140	35
141	35
142	35
143	35

Proverbs

8:10	8
16:6	75
22:11	80
26:11	122

Ecclesiastes

5:4–5	33–34

Isaiah

1:12–17	19–20
6:5	75
6:6	74
12:5–6	18
43:23–24	23
53:7	77
53:10b–11	63
65:2–5	58

Jeremiah

7:18	21
11:13	21
19:1–7	21
19:5	65
31:7	18
44:25	21

Ezekiel

6:13	21
8:6	48
10:18–19	48–49
11:6	49
11:16–20	49
11:22–23	49
20:25	1–2
20:26	2
20:28	21
21:21	36
23:38–39	21
36:18–19	46
37:23	46
43:1–5	56
43:7	56
43:18–26	42
45:18–20	42

Hosea

11:2	21

Amos

4:4–5	20
5:21–24	20
5:22	67

Zechariah

13:2	80

Malachi

1:6–14	23

Scripture Index

(Malachi continued)

1:11	71
3:8–11	33

Matthew

5:17	6
5:21–48	6
5:23–24	6, 25, 61
8:2–4	6, 25
9:20–21	88
9:23–25	88
12:1–8	7
21:12–13	11
21:14	25
21:23	25
22:32	53
22:34–40	132
23:23	6
26:26	69
26:27	69
26:55	25

Mark

1:21–26	11
1:40–44	6, 25
2:23–28	6
3:1–5	6
5:24–28	88
5:38–41	88
7	129
7:1–23	132
7:1–5	85
7:15–23	85–86
7:22	46
11:15–17	11
11:27	25
12:35	25
12:41–44	70
14:22	69
14:23	69
14:24	43
14:49	25

Luke

5:12–14	6, 25
5:14	42
6:1–5	6
7:2–5	25
7:12–14	88
8:42–44	88
8:52–54	88
10:30–32	87
13:10–17	6
14:1–6	6
17:12–14	6, 25
19:45–46	11
19:47	25
20:1	25
21:1–4	70
21:37–38	25
22:19	69
22:20	69
22:42	66
22:53	25

John

1:29	43, 76
2:6	94
2:13–16	11
3:16	38
4:7–18	88
4:16–18	85
4:19–24	132
5:2–17	6
7:14	25
8:2	25
8:3–11	88
8:20	25
8:28	66
10:23	25
12:20–21	25
18:20	25
19:31–33	77

Acts

2:46	25
3:1	25
5:12–21	25
5:42	25
10:1–2	25
10:11–16	129
15:22–29	52
16:13	94

Scripture Index

16:14	25
17:23	63
18:7	25
21:17–26	25
22:16	123

Romans

1:28	2
3:24	43
3:31	7
5:10	43
6:3–4	123
6:23	113
7:12	7
8:31	63

1 Corinthians

7:19	131
11:23–24	69
11:25	69

2 Corinthians

5:17–21	63
5:18	43

Galatians

1:4	43
2:20	43
3:13	43
4:5	43

Ephesians

5:2	43
5:19	18

Philippians

2:6–8	66

Colossians

1:20	43
3:16	18

1 Timothy

2:6	43

Titus

3:9	132

Hebrews

2:10	69
8:1—10:25	7
9:1—10:22	63
9:1—10:18	43
9:14	43
9:22	42
9:26	66
9:28	43
10:3	4
10:19–22	63, 66–67

James

1:8	122

1 Peter

1:18	43
2:5	117
2:24	43
3:20–21	123

Revelation

1:5	43
5:6	77
5:9	43
7:14	63

www.ingramcontent.com/pod-product-compliance
Lightning Source LLC
Chambersburg PA
CBHW071433160426
43195CB00013B/1882